Pelican Books

From Hand to Mouth

Marianne Herzog was born in Mecklenburg in the DDR in 1939. At the age of fifteen she began a three-year apprenticeship in a State-owned bookshop, and in 1957, prior to the construction of the Wall, she moved to West Germany. She worked and travelled in the West for over two years before returning to the DDR. She did not stay for long, however, and eventually settled in West Germany for a second time.

There then followed a succession of jobs – in a children's home, as a bookseller, in a remand home for girls and, finally, as a factory worker. She first began writing about her experiences in the remand home, and this resulted in a sixty-minute radio programme. She subsequently wrote further programmes on prostitution and on prisons. However, it is her experiences as a factory pieceworker, the job at which she spent the longest time, that serve as the basis for this book.

Marianne Herzog

From Hand to Mouth

Women and Piecework

Translated by Stanley Mitchell

Penguin Books

Penguin Books Ltd, Harmondsworth,
Middlesex, England
Penguin Books, 625 Madison Avenue,
New York, New York 10022, U.S.A.
Penguin Books Australia Ltd, Ringwood,
Victoria, Australia
Penguin Books Canada Ltd, 2801 John Street,
Markham, Ontario, Canada L3R 1B4
Penguin Books (N.Z.) Ltd, 182–190 Wairau Road,
Auckland 10, New Zealand

First published in West Germany as *Von der Hand in den Mund* by
Rotbuch Verlag 1976
English translation with new Introduction and Postscript first
published 1980

The publishers wish to thank Allison & Busby Ltd
for permission to publish 'Song of the Cotton-Pickers',
from B. Traven, *The Cotton-Pickers* (copyright © B. Traven
and R. E. Luján, 1969)

Typeset, printed and bound in Great Britain by
Hazell Watson & Viney Ltd, Aylesbury, Bucks
Set in Monotype Ehrhardt

Contents

Contents

Introduction
by Sally Alexander

From Hand to Mouth describes how things are made and the lives of the women who make them. It is an account of women's unskilled factory work in West Germany – and in West Germany 94 per cent of women factory workers are 'unskilled'. Marianne Herzog describes the work she herself did in Berlin, Munich and other cities in the Federal Republic: spot-welding tubes for TV and radio, assembling vacuum cleaners, packing olives and spare parts for lorries. The brand-names of the multi-national companies which employ women are as familiar as the household goods which they produce – Siemens, Electrolux, Gillette and others. Equally familiar throughout Western Europe and the USA, indeed every capitalist economy, are the characteristics of the women workers – low-paid, unskilled, poorly organized. Such is the effectiveness of the division of labour and the separation of classes in Western economies, so completely does the operation of the market (that is, the paraphernalia of distribution and exchange) dominate the visible world and conceal the world of work, that those who do not work in factories know little or nothing about them. *From Hand to Mouth* disturbs this ignorance. Marianne Herzog reaches beyond the language and categories of official statistics to describe the experience of work which those statistics conceal. She itemizes the details of the labour process itself, the composition of the working day and the methods of payment which divide a workforce already divided by sex, language and cultural differences. She describes the isolation of a pieceworker and the strain of reaching a required piece-number minute after minute. A series of almost cinematic images, in a clipped, sparse prose, takes us into different work-

7

shops, and through a working day. *From Hand to Mouth* is a convincing indictment of the organization of work under modern industrial capitalism, and in particular of the division of labour which places women and immigrants at the bottom of the job hierarchy.

Because it is a first-hand description of a series of labour processes, *From Hand to Mouth* makes an original and thoughtful contribution to the literature of women's work. It begins to fill a void in our knowledge of capitalist production: the experience of the people who make the goods which we and they consume. But Marianne Herzog is not a typical factory worker. She does not speak for the other women with whom she worked. She writes of her own experience and her viewpoint is a distinctive one, that of a socialist and a feminist.

Marianne Herzog was trained as a bookshop worker in the German Democratic Republic. After going to West Germany she took work in engineering because she had to earn money to live, but also because she wanted to learn about women's factory work – what women earn and what they produce. She deliberately avoided what were more conspicuously women's jobs: 'I did not want to be an unskilled childminder, an unskilled salesgirl in a department store or an unskilled orderly in a hospital. I didn't want to be a waitress or a cleaner.' Later, after working in the factories, she wanted to communicate the experiences of work itself, because, as she writes in her Foreword, 'If we are to fight this kind of work – which becomes no more than a few turns of the wrist, if we are to fight this working-to-the-bone, this having to produce five to twelve items a minute for eight hours at a time, we also have to describe it.'

Immanent in her dissection of a working day is a sharp but controlled anger at the way those who actually produce the goods – the vast majority of them women – spend their lives. Too exhausted, drained, enervated to resist the dictates of the factory, these women become mere flexible appendages to the machine.

Their labour, in Marianne Herzog's view, is forced labour; the metaphor of the prison is present throughout the text. *From Hand to Mouth*, then, is both a critical description of the capitalist labour process and part of Marianne Herzog's own story of survival. It is a fragment towards the understanding of the collective experience of work – an experience which at present is largely absent from our language, culture and political practice. Through its detailed but unadorned reportage of what factory work on a production line means, each day and each week, *From Hand to Mouth* graphically reveals the ways in which capitalist production utilizes women's subordination in the mechanisms of exploitation.

It is this emphasis upon the actual process of production and what the wage relationship means for most women factory workers that sets Marianne Herzog's book apart from the growing number of official, academic and journalistic inquiries into women's employment that have been piling up in the last decade. This curiosity is in part a response to the increase all over the Western world in the number of women, especially married women, going *out* to work since the end of the Second World War. But it has also been provoked by the resurgence of militant feminism, the Women's Liberation Movement, from the late 1960s onwards. It was mainly in response to this international phenomenon that the United Nations declared 1975 International Women's Year, an event which in turn gave rise to an epidemic of surveys of women's work. Such miscellaneous bodies as the ILO, the OECD and the EEC, as well as the employment departments of respective governments, have all recently issued information, together with a host of more modest reports from trade union research bodies and employers' organizations.

Despite manifest differences in political inspiration and purpose, these surveys characterize women's work and women's place in society in very similar ways. They derive their authority from national statistics of population and employment, which,

9

Introduction

together with the application of conventionally accepted socio-logical categories, construct both the patterns of female employ-ment and social attitudes. The picture which they present of women's work informs government policy (such as it is), per-meates the media, and to a greater or lesser extent informs the way that employers, many trade unionists, and even sectors of feminist opinion think about women and women's work. Because this view of women's waged work is the dominant one, it is worth identifying its central features.

Women and work: the conventional view

Whatever their initial inspiration, most surveys in the past ten years have focused their attention upon women's 'inequality' at work. While this inequality is of course condemned, it is generally placed in a positive long-term context. The opening observation is that more women than ever are entering the labour force and, with some reservations, this is welcomed as a sign of progress. The ILO, for example, in its 1974 report on the position of women workers, notes that there has been 'a considerable improvement in the status of women workers in many countries in different parts of the world, together with a heightened aware-ness of the need for women to have equality of opportunity and treatment with men in the world of work'.[1] Progress is measured not only by women's increased economic activity but also by the arrival in our streets of policewomen and traffic wardens, not to mention the oft-cited case of Sweden's women crane-drivers.

The reports then, however, go on to catalogue the characteris-tics of inequality, which identify women as an under-privileged sector of the labour market: low pay, lack of status and mono-tonous jobs in a narrow range of occupations. 'Women's work' is defined most succinctly in Robert Gubber's report to an

1. ILO, *Equality of Opportunity and Treatment for Women Workers*, Geneva, 1974, p. 77

OECD trade union seminar in 1968:[2] it is 'unskilled' . . . calling for 'great resilience', 'manual dexterity'; it is fragmented and purely operative; it is poorly paid; it involves no responsibilities. The conclusion is that at present there is still no proper integration of women in the labour market – they still form a marginal or reserve labour force.

Some hope in this situation is pinned on technical advance, which is welcomed as offering new 'opportunities' for women's work participation, although 'mechanization' is greeted more guardedly: 'Certain branches of activity are becoming more "feminine" in that they require a lower level of skill owing to the introduction of more highly mechanized production methods.'[3] But the real motors of progressive change, as far as women's new economic opportunities are concerned, are seen as demographic and cultural:

More women are married: they marry younger; they increasingly have all their children before they are 30; they have fewer children; they have access to more domestic appliances which aid housework; they are increasingly better educated and are acquiring more skills and qualifications; and they have increasingly strong incentives to earn and achieve a higher standard of living for their families. With changing social attitudes, women with higher educational qualifications, and there are increasingly more of them, tend to have personal aspirations for their career advancement, pay and status of employment.[4]

The only clouds on the horizon of increasing opportunities for waged work are outdated prejudices on the part of society,

2. Robert Gubber, 'Characteristics of Supply and Demand for Women Workers on the Labour Market', in *The Employment of Women* (Final Report of Regional Trade Union Seminar), OECD, Paris, 1970, p. 106

3. F. Guéland Léridon, General Report, in *The Employment of Women* (see note 2), p. 27

4. Department of Employment, Manpower Paper No. 12, *Women and Work: Overseas Practice*, p. 2

employers, trade unions, men, and even women themselves. The suggestion is that the problem begins not at work but with sex-role stereotyping at school, and there's a strong emphasis on parental responsibility. According to the 1975 OECD Report, for example: 'The easy logic of each step a girl takes towards her vocational future – each proceeding naturally from all previous steps back to her earliest handling by her parents – is a powerful clarifier in understanding the basis for many of the problems a woman encounters in entering the labour market.'[5] Women themselves are also chastised for their lack of ambition and their too ready acceptance of their own inferiority. Men's hostility to women's entry into new spheres of employment is matched by women's diffidence. Thus the same OECD Report argues with some exasperation that women's persistent educational inferiority cannot wholly be explained by 'discrimination': 'an alternative explanation must be considered . . . [that] women . . . in the nature of things, have been conditioned to expect the role of wife and mother – or perhaps of teacher, nurse or secretary before marriage and children – and . . . have been discouraged from thoughts of a life-long working career.'[6] Women's low expectations, then, their lack of drive and ambition, perpetuate inequality and provoke discrimination; and these expectations are part of women's conditioning which stems from the 'nature of things'.

The remedies proposed are legislative reform of discriminatory practices at work and school, and changes in women's legal status. Some venture the possibility of the socialization of housework, but the real emphasis is laid on vocational guidance and training for girls and women to enable them to seize the new opportunities opening before them in industry and to help them overcome their own sense of inadequacy and inferiority. Since it is the resolute purpose of the surveys to enlighten public opinion,

5. OECD, *The Role of Women in the Economy*, 1975, p. 51
6. OECD, op. cit., pp. 47–8

employers, trade unionists and women alike are exhorted to change their ideas and attitudes.

The utility of these surveys lies in the information they provide as well as the occasional random insight. One or two are worth looking at for the knowledge and thought of a particular compiler or author (for example, Evelyne Sullerot in *The Employment of Women*, the Final Report of the 1968 OECD Trade Union Seminar).[7] Nevertheless, while the description of women's work is, in its essentials, accurate, as a full explanation of women's inequality vis à vis men on the labour market, the analysis is inadequate. It never properly probes beneath the surface phenomena of inequality. This is not to suggest that a fiction of women's work has been deliberately or wilfully constructed, but that the picture presented is incomplete. Discrimination and inequality are dealt with as they operate in the market place, but the world of social production is never investigated as a source of divisions and inequalities among the working class. Thus, technical innovation is mentioned as providing 'opportunities' for female employment; mechanization is held responsible for the 'feminization' of many jobs; women's 'dual role' is invoked as an explanation for the low-paid, part-time character of married women's work. But the methods of work and payment, the division of labour and hierarchy of jobs – in other words, the relations of production and the labour process itself – are never carefully examined. In economic terms, the weight of explanation for women's lack of status as waged workers is placed almost unilaterally on the supply side. Responsibility for the character and quality of women's work is laid at the door of 'society', particularly its homes, its schools and its legal codes. It is 'society' which deposits poor-quality female labour at the factory gates. It is never sufficiently questioned how far the structure of advanced capitalist production depends upon the large-scale availability of cheap unskilled

7. See note 2

Introduction

labour, and who, therefore, would do 'women's work' if women ceased to do it.

One reason for this neglect is the vast generality of the project. Because women workers exhibit similar features across continents – that is, they have children, sometimes husbands, and always domestic as well as waged work – the canvas on which they are surveyed can be literally world-wide. The project of the ILO in the early 1970s, for instance, aimed to 'bring up to date the report on women workers in a changing world, with particular reference to identifying the needs relating to equal opportunity and treatment and the problems arising from rapidly changing structures and conditions of work.'[8]

The report, while inviting admiration for its attempt to comprehend one half of the human race in a single empirical category, nevertheless fails to convince. Women throughout the world are divided by differences of race, religion and culture; they inhabit social relations of production and kinship in different historical contexts. Most international surveys sensibly confine themselves more modestly to parts of Western Europe and the USA, casting only sidelong glances elsewhere. But even these, while noting uneven economic development from nation to nation, tend to describe them simply as more 'backward' or 'advanced', depending on whether they retain a strong agrarian sector, and on the relative status of the manufacturing and service (or tertiary) sectors. The dominant picture is of a series of nations moving haltingly but inevitably through successive stages of backwardness towards advanced status, opening up new opportunities for female waged work as they proceed. A direct relationship is assumed, then, between women and economic development. The sexual division of labour, a social relationship between men and women (which assumes many different shapes in different economic, political and ideological

8. ILO, *Equality of Opportunity and Treatment for Women Workers*, Geneva, 1974, p. 1

14

structures) is confused with sexual difference defined by biology. Thus the distinct social–sexual relations of women and men, both in the family and at work, are obscured by a functionalist notion of social 'roles' which allegedly flow from biology (women's reproductive capacity) on the one hand, and technological innovation (mechanization) on the other. Because the social space vacated by the family and production is filled by biology and technology, any further scrutiny is inhibited. Both biology and technology are treated as natural or at least asocial phenomena, and as such remain unquestioned.

In the combined presence of progressive technology and biological inevitability, the source of 'inequality' can only be attributed to backward attitudes and expectations, residues of 'the past', or of 'tradition'. Thus those obstinate and tenacious problems for feminism – how do ideas about women's place come about and change, and how do we, men and women, internalize those ideas? What are the historical determinants of the sexual division of labour, and in what ways is sexual difference socially constructed through the sexual division of labour? – these problems and questions, the terrain of feminism, are simply obliterated. If attitudes and expectations are simply old-fashioned ideas then they can be legislated away.

Legislative reform and the sexual division of labour

However desirable in themselves, the recommended reforms (where they have been introduced) leave untouched the place of women in social production. The Equal Pay Act in Britain is a case in point. The Act (introduced by Barbara Castle, Labour Minister of Employment, passed in 1970 and brought into force in 1975) stipulates that, for the law to be operative, women's work must be the same as, broadly similar to, or of equal value to that of men. This definition immediately excludes an estimated three million women workers in the segregated, low-paid, all-female occupations. To be eligible for equal pay, women workers must have men with whom to compare themselves. Even where this is the case, however, the Act offers no simple panacea. Men's jobs are graded more highly than women's in job evaluation or other grading schemes. If women (as individuals or groups) believe their jobs are comparable and of equal value to men's, the responsibility rests with them to take their cases to an Industrial Tribunal. The success-rate at Tribunals is not high. Of the 363 cases heard in 1977, only 25 per cent were successful.[9]

When women workers have achieved an equal basic rate with men, their earnings will be lower. Domestic responsibilities prevent overtime work, much shift-work, bonuses for long service (which some white-collar unions have negotiated), and promotion.

Only through collective bargaining have women workers in some cases established parity with men's rates of pay, and this has usually only been achieved with the support of male workers. For, as the history of successful claims shows, women must remain vigilant lest, on the one hand, their jobs are regraded and they find themselves at the bottom of a new integrated grading system, or, on the other hand, the employers replace them with male workers. In their struggle for equal pay, women must not only combat the resourceful tactics of their employers – when the Equal Pay Act was first introduced the Confederation of British Industry issued a brochure entitled *13 Ways to Avoid the Equal Pay Act*, which has been widely used – but must also fight men's resistance to the notion of parity with 'women's work'. The point is not to argue against legislative reforms, which can be a useful if limited weapon, but to insist that by themselves legislative reforms will leave untouched the deeper causes of inequality. Furthermore, anti-discriminatory legislation, like protective legislation (the justification of which was

9. *Department of Employment Gazette*, April 1978

that women were incapable of self-protection), is no substitute for the collective self-activity of women workers. The Equal Pay Act in Britain deliberately eschews this possibility by forcing a direct relationship between the individual and legal redress.

To summarize the conventional mental picture of the relationship between women, waged work and inequality: legislative reform is only a temporary if necessary expedient, because the real harbingers of change in women's social and economic position are the new opportunities for waged work, the effect of progressive industrialization. The implication is that as more and more women enter paid employment outside the home, the older rigidities in the sexual division of labour (including out-of-date attitudes) are being whittled away. This faith in the essential benevolence of industrialization and the power of rational thought to eliminate prejudice and injustice has a long and respectable lineage. It is reminiscent of neo-classical political economy. Perhaps the most influential and indeed persuasive exponent of this view is Viola Klein, whose many studies of women workers in the years since the end of the Second World War have helped to shape both official and common-sense views of women's place on the labour market:

At the beginning of industrialization, they [women] were largely employed as unskilled factory hands (and, of course, in domestic service) ... with the development of light industry and of subsidiary services, they entered semi-skilled and white-collar occupations; during the latest phase of industrial development, they can be found in substantial numbers in executive jobs and are providing the personnel for most ancillary professions, such as medicine, law, accountancy, journalism, etc. Each new stage has, of course, not superseded the previous one, but at each phase another layer was added to the preceding ones and new opportunities were created for female employment.[10]

Viola Klein allows for the influence of feminism, or at least of

10. V. Klein, *Britain's Married Women Workers*, Routledge & Kegan Paul, 1965; 1968 edition, p. 14

17

women's own desires, on their improved social and economic status, but undoubtedly the central stimulus to emancipation is the lure of the factory: 'Work in factories, offices, shops, etc. is alluring to married women (the single ones being already fully employed) who are not sufficiently occupied at home and many of whom feel socially isolated.'

The myopic refusal to confront capitalist production as a harsh mode of exploitation which perpetually reproduces inequalities through division of labour, work discipline, the wage relation itself, ultimately prohibits this school of thought from leading to the eradication of inequality. Marianne Herzog's book, deceptively simple in its language and in the stories it tells, offers its readers a quite different understanding of the economic and political boundaries of women's working lives. For her, factory work is a particularly pernicious form of work for women. But, before examining what is distinctive in Marianne Herzog's approach, I propose to pursue the theme of the historical relationship between women's work and capitalist industry, in order to question the belief that industrial capitalism in itself emancipates women.

The increase in women's employment

Increasing numbers of married women are going out to work in most West European economies and the USA. In Britain, for instance, almost 40 per cent of the labour force is female and nearly two thirds of these are married. Or, to put it another way, there are almost six million married women workers in the 1970s, compared with just under one million forty years ago. An increasing number of these women have children under five and research shows that more mothers of young children would go out to work if there were adequate provision for childcare. According to the *Economist* (18 May 1978) married women are the growth sector of the labour force at the present time. But is this a sign of progress or of women's changing role? Since the origins of wage labour, wives and mothers have contributed to the family income whenever work is available, domestic responsibilities permit and economic need dictates. The recorded increase in married women's work in Britain in the past twenty years is evidence that more and more families are dependent on two incomes. The increasing proportion of married women in the labour market in the past five years or so must be set in the context of increasing male unemployment. The evidence suggests that women workers have been introduced into some sectors of the economy, particularly many branches of manufacturing industry, to pull the general level of wages downward. The picture is a complex and difficult one to interpret, but there is no evidence that the increase in married women's waged work is in itself an indication either of improved status or of changing role.

What is changing, however, is work organization and work methods. Much of the work that women once performed in their own or somebody else's home has been transformed, or rather reorganized, by the intervention of the market. Until the Second World War, for instance, many married women took in washing or took it to the local baths to wash; women still wash other people's clothes, but nowadays they do it in launderettes or laundries. Similarly, today there are more office cleaners working for contract cleaning companies, and waitresses, maids and cleaners in hotels and restaurants, than there are domestic servants in private houses. Women are doing the work they have always done, only now they are employed by a firm or company, their hours of work and methods of payment are to some extent regularized, their relationship to the state through taxation and national insurance more formalized. In these ways married women's waged work has become more visible. The rapid expansion of the service sector in most capitalist economies has been mainly responsible for the filling out of the statistics of

Introduction

women's economic activity rates in the Censuses since 1945.
But what this marks is the extension of commodity production,
not a change in women's role.

Women's place in industry: women as 'cheap labour'

Historically, female labour has always provided a strategic source
of cheap labour for industrial capital in its restless search to
maximize profit and reduce costs. The breakdown of handicraft
skill into separate tasks and the introduction of machinery and
cheap labour are the fundamental principles of modern industry.
But this tendency of capital to reorganize skill is hindered by the
resistance of the workforce whenever possible. Control over
workshop practices by the workmen themselves was the phenomenon identified and abhorred by Frederick William Taylor,
high priest of scientific management, in the Pennsylvania Mid-
vale Steel Company in the late nineteenth century. Distressed to
discover that workshop practices were determined by custom
and rule of thumb, that men learned their jobs and acquired
knowledge by watching others, he wanted to eliminate industrial
inefficiency, that is, 'the old system of management', whereby
'each workman shall be left with the final responsibility for
doing his job practically as he thinks best, with comparatively
little help and advice from management'.[11] He urged that
management's task must be to appropriate the collective knowledge of the entire workforce, collate and tabulate it, and then
reissue it to the workers in the form of written instructions.
Management should also select and train the workforce carefully,
encourage competition between workers and bargain with each
one separately.

These two principles represent the 'science' in scientific
management. They attempt to systematize and legitimate the

11. F. W. Taylor, *The Principles of Scientific Management*, New York and
London, 1911, p. 15

logic of capital, ease the advance of modern industry by the
seizure of real control over the labour process, and provide the
ideology of 'rationalization' elaborated since. Ideally, skills are
concentrated into special departments under the supervision
and instruction of layers of management. (Henry Ford: 'I have
put skill into management planning and building and the results
are enjoyed by the unskilled.') The workforce is carefully
selected and graded with the majority of manual workers –
indeed almost all of them – ignorant of the work outside their
shop or department. (The Lip worker cited by Marianne Herzog,
for instance, only discovered which part of a clock she was
making because she made a special point of finding out during
a factory occupation.) The entry of female labour into an
industry has also been part of the employers' strategy to reduce
costs, an accompaniment to the fragmentation of skills and the
'degradation of work', to use Harry Braverman's phrase.

The classic instance of this process, the use of women in textile
factories in the Industrial Revolution, is well known. Another
example is the conversion of the engineering industry during the
First World War to the mass production of armaments. Women
had to be trained rapidly for productive work from the end of
1914. They were drawn in from the more orthodox 'female
trades': dressmakers and milliners' assistants, laundry workers,
textile workers, confectionery workers, light metal workers,
together with recruits from domestic service and the sweated
trades. Work was subdivided, women performing one or two
tasks under male supervision to start with, moving on to more
complicated processes as they progressed in skill and training.
But the majority of women were employed on simple repetitive
operations: 'We put the brains into the machines before the
women begin' was how one manager of a shell factory described
it.

The principles of 'dilution', as the progressive replacement of
skilled men by women and machinery was known, were enshrined

in the Treasury Agreement of March 1915, an agreement made between the employers, the government and representatives from the skilled men's unions. Women workers, the principle object of the negotiations, were not present at the meeting, nor were their interests represented. It was not until July 1915 that the National Federation of Women Workers (NFWW), under the leadership of Mary MacArthur, reached a working alliance with the largest skilled engineers' union, the Amalgamated Society of Engineers (ASE). Its terms echoed the main points of the Treasury Agreement, and it was subsequently followed by agreements with craft unions in other trades. The ASE agreed to cooperate with the introduction of women workers into their shops, provided that women received 'the rate for the job', and that they undertook to leave men's jobs at the end of the war. In practice, female labour, where it replaced that of skilled or semi-skilled men, was introduced through negotiations with rank-and-file or union representatives on the shop-floor.

Between 1918 and 1922, women were thrown out of most of the jobs which they had not occupied before the war. They were expected to return to domestic service or the home. The next mass introduction of female labour into manufacturing industry occurred with the development of the 'new industries' in the inter-war years – characterized by J. B. Priestley as 'potato crisps, scent, toothpastes, bathing costumes, fire extinguishers, radios, soap, clothes and a hundred other things'. Because these were years of economic depression and unemployment, entre-preneurs could dictate their terms. British industry was restruc-tured (experienced its second 'industrial revolution') while the Labour Movement was on the defensive. Industrialists borrowed the techniques of mass production learned in wartime and drew on fresh supplies of cheap labour. Referring to the new indus-tries in a government inquiry, the Board of Trade spokesman stated:

Industries using automatic or semi-automatic machinery and requiring for the most part only semi-skilled labour have tended to become established in districts with adequate supplies of labour with the necessary experience or with the reputation for adaptability. Often female or juvenile labour has been thought to be suitable for such industries.[12]

A report to the ILO in 1936 went so far as to argue that the employment of women in these jobs was a 'technical necessity' ... 'their delicacy of touch is indispensable for a large number of tasks in which most men would be completely incapable or deplorably inferior.'[13] Women's manual dexterity and quickness of eye, their delicacy and lightness of touch, made them cleaner, neater and quicker at noticing defects, sewing up bags, assembling and packaging goods and minding machines. Fuss's view has found endless repetition in the subsequent literature. Femininity is apparently a special qualification for repetitive, sedentary, monotonous occupations.

Women workers have thus served as a cheap, flexible and docile labour supply for capitalist industry, both in the 'old' manufacturing trades - textiles, clothing, printing and others - where they displaced skilled men and in the 'new' industries - light engineering, food processing and, today, electronics. The expansion of the service sector, characteristic of capitalist economies since the Second World War, has similarly been built on the subdivision of labour, the fragmentation of skills, the separation of mental and manual labour, and the employment of women and girls. (The expansion in part-time work underlines the flexibility of these grades of labour.) The two principle ways in which the sexual division of labour is structured in modern industry are therefore the following: first, the

12. Board of Trade Evidence to the Barlow Commission, para. 87
13. Henry Fuss, *Unemployment and Employment among Women*, ILO, Geneva, 1936, p. 31

Introduction

concentration of women in a few industries – in Britain in 1974,
60 per cent of all female employees were in occupations where
more than three quarters of all employees were female;[14] and
second, the restriction of women to low-paid unskilled work.

Skilled men and exclusion

Some feminists in search of an explanation for this ghetto-ization
of women workers, and for the seemingly unbreakable connec-
tion between women's work, low pay and lack of skill, have
claimed that this relationship is the result of women's exclusion
from skilled work by men's unions. (Millicent Garret Fawcett,
President of the National Union of Women's Suffrage Societies
until 1918, was deeply attached to this view.) And the history of
the British trade union movement to some extent supports this
belief. 'Between skilled and unskilled workers a gulf is fixed,'
wrote Thomas Wright, a journeyman engineer, in the 1860s, and
the gulf was unbridgeable between skilled men and female
labour. Skilled men, defending the customs of their craft from
the depredations of 'rationalization', regarded with fear and
contempt the demands of women workers or their union leaders
for entry into skilled work during the First World War. 'Industrial feminism is full of menace to the labour movement,' wrote
G. D. H. Cole, Guild Socialist, leading member of the Labour
Party and spokesman for the ASE, in 1917.

   Despite the fact that the concept and application of skill have
been revolutionized continually since the time when handicraft
was the technical basis of the mode of production and the 'mys-
teries' of the trade which shrouded a craftsman in prestige were
the collective property of the handicraft workers, union organization and collective bargaining in Britain still lean heavily on
this notion that an identity of interest among a group of workers

14. Department of Employment. Manpower Paper No. 9, *Women and
Work: A Statistical Survey,* 1974, p. 22

is established through common practice of, if not exclusive possession of, a skill. 'Exclusion', or at least segregation, remains a principle of organization in many trade unions. The survival of craft consciousness is part of the legacy of Britain's position as the first industrial nation, the 'workshop of the world'. Even the unionization of the weakest workers can be thought through in craft terms. When, for instance, night cleaners were attempting to organize in 1971–3, they were advised by the secretary of the window-cleaners' branch of the Transport and General Workers' Union that the first step towards self-help was to establish a skill.

While industrial self-protection inevitably involves recognition of occupational distinctions between one group of workers and another, men's resistance to women workers is in part a response to the ways in which women workers have been used as blacklegs or scabs to undercut men's skills and rates of pay. Therefore skilled men have sought to protect their interests through excluding women always from formal apprenticeship and often from union membership. This, however, is an effect, not the cause, of women's structurally weak position on the labour market.

It is easier to describe women's work than to speculate how change might come about, because the sexual division of labour is a historical relationship which structures both economic relations and unconscious mental processes. Marianne Herzog does not address herself directly to these questions. But implicit in her text is a two-fold explanation of women's especial vulnerability as waged workers. The first aspect is to be seen in the emphasis that she places upon piecework.

Introduction

Piecework

For Marianne Herzog, piecework, characteristic of women's work in manufacturing industry, underlines and perpetuates women's vulnerability as waged workers. Seventy per cent of all women factory workers in the Federal Republic are on piece-work, and for them it means an eight-hour day (or longer) with unpaid breaks for lunch and tea, visits to the lavatory or to collect raw materials or equipment – unpaid because a piece-worker is only paid for the time spent producing at the machine. Piecework means that wages have to be beaten out of the machines, often with the aid of painkillers, that women work so close to the machines that they almost seem to 'crawl into them'. It means a work cycle of a few seconds, sometimes more, but always under a minute. These are the conditions described by Marianne Herzog and they are echoed throughout British industry.[15]

Worn out or fed up, pieceworkers can always leave. They will be replaced by young school-leavers or immigrants willing to work for much lower wages. Most large towns have a pool of unemployed or under-employed women workers, many of whom are immigrants (West Indian, Asian and Irish in North London, for instance). During a recession the numbers will multiply.

To the naïve or uninitiated, piecework appears the most rational and indeed equitable method of payment because wages are seemingly directly related to output. For this reason Marx

15. The term 'piecework' is used loosely throughout industry and designates many different methods of payment by results. Often methods of pay are so complicated that it is difficult for the wage-earner to follow them. The widespread method for women workers in British light engineering is a basic rate with piece-rates above that. I could obtain no information about methods of payment prevalent in the engineering industry in the Federal Republic from the German labour attaché. Indeed the Embassy could give me no information at all about the conditions of women workers.

described piecework as the method of payment most in harmony with capital. In fact the distinction between piece and time wages is more apparent than real, since piece-rates (or any form of payment by results) are calculated on a time basis – so much has to be produced in a given time, with some form of reward if the output is faster.

For employers, piece-rates have a pleasing simplicity in that they offer an incentive to the worker to work harder; the faster the output, the higher the earnings, or so it seems. In the language of late-nineteenth-century neo-classical economics, the efficient labourer will raise his or her wages by 'a superior intensity of exertion'. Piecework therefore controls the quantity and intensity of work, and it achieves this through the self-supervision of the worker. Persuading workers to contribute voluntarily a 'superior intensity of exertion' is at the heart of all productivity deals, even if businessmen in pursuit of good public relations often like to imply that it is about something quite different. For instance, according to Jack Greenborough, Deputy Chairman of Shell UK and President of the CBI, 'There is a mistaken notion that "productivity" is all about making people work harder. It is not. It is about equipping, organizing and motivating them to work more effectively.'[16]

For women workers in the engineering industry in the FDR, the incentive to work hard is produced by the basic rate being set beneath subsistence. The effort necessary to push earnings comfortably above subsistence is neither constant nor predictable. The women who work fastest to push up their earnings not only have their piece-rates re-assessed and subsequently reduced but wear themselves out in the process. Furthermore, piece-rates are calculated in such a way that payment per piece decreases proportionately as output rises. In this way extra effort replenishes capital, while the costs of that extra effort (the strain on physical and mental health that it involves) are borne by

16. Quoted in the *Sunday Times*, 2 July 1978

Introduction

the pieceworker. For instance, the method of payment by results that operates on an assembly line in a North London light engineering firm was described to me as follows:

[During the dispute] . . . we discovered that to reach the basic rate we only have to produce one third of what is actually produced during the day. But the workers have no control over the number of instruments they do; when the light flashes, the operator at the front of the line puts out a tray with two instruments in it onto the line. The frequency of the light flashing is set by the chargehand and there is a laid-down interval between flashes for each set. For example, on the Princess, the light flashed every two minutes, and we did 60 an hour, whereas on the Maxi there were 36 trays an hour, which means 72 instruments an hour and 576 a day. This system enables the firm to have two thirds of its speedos assembled for about £6 per week per operator.[17]

In theory, the piece-rate is agreed between workers and management. In practice, there can be no bargain between management and unorganized workers. A rate-fixer, trained in work-study techniques, is brought in by the management to time the workers' actions and measure their 'effort'. New piece-rates are then imposed in the ways described by Marianne Herzog. The rates are set individually and at strategic moments in the year (busy periods before holidays and Christmas, for example), thus further undermining workers' resistance to them.

Because it presupposes the separation, organization and measurement of tasks to the point where all initiative on the part of the worker is eliminated, piecework of this kind is especially applicable on the production lines of consumer goods industries where mass production of a standardized product permits such methods of work and payment. These are the manufacturing industries we have already identified as those in which women predominate: clothing, textiles, electrical goods,

17. Miriam Glucksmann, unpublished MS., 1978

light engineering, food processing, the tobacco trade, etc.
Despite significant differences in the methods of work in each
industry, the sexual division on the shop-floor has a remarkable
uniformity. Many examples could be given; typical is this
situation in a London toy factory, described by an English
feminist:

Of the 2,000 women, about half work on assembly lines and half on
individual machines. Both are run on a 'basic rate plus piecework'
basis. The men are all mechanics, chargehands, etc., except for the
skilled men in the toolroom and the semi-skilled men in the foundry
and tumblers. The men and women are completely divided by job
categories and rates of pay.[18]

Piecework of the type described by Marianne Herzog is,
however, again a symptom rather than a cause of women's
industrial weakness, for what distinguishes women's work from
men's is not piecework *per se*, but the low level of earnings
which that system of payment in the case of women reinforces
and perpetuates. Of the size of this differential there can be no
doubt. In England before the First World War, the average
wage of a woman manual worker was one third to one half of a
man's. Today the average hourly earnings of women manual
workers are just over 60 per cent of men's. Many women workers
in offices, shops and launderettes, as well as factories, earn less
than 50p per hour, and those who do not have a man's wage to
help support themselves and their children take two jobs or
work overtime to make ends meet.

The principal justification for women's low wages has always
been that women's earnings are only supplementary to family
income. It is indeed the supplementary character of much
women's work which explains the general rate at which their
wages are set. But this justification wholly ignores the large
number of households which are supported primarily or entirely

18. *Red Rag*, No. 11

Introduction

by women. The 1971 Census showed that nearly two million women under retirement age were the chief economic supporters of their households. To recognize the claims of these women would be to contradict the dominant familial ideology. The idea of women as dependents has not only justified private industry's gross underpayment of women workers, but has also informed the trade unions' demand for a family wage and is fundamental to the social security system and, indeed, the whole apparatus of the welfare state. Most important, perhaps, it has often prevented women themselves from organizing to demand higher wages or equal pay with men.

Women workers and the family

If methods of payment cannot in themselves be considered a cause of women's industrial situation, the second source of women's vulnerability as wage workers emphasized by Marianne Herzog – their position in the family – certainly can. Commodity production dictates the forms of wage work available to women, but the 'ties' they experience – their children, other dependents and domestic work – 'force' women's economic dependence on the factory. The focus of *From Hand to Mouth* is wage work – the world of the factory – but underlying the factory is the other world of the family. The account of the family in the book exhibits the familiar ambivalence of feminism towards the home, domestic work and relationships within the family. On the one hand the family is the source of love and warmth and human relationships, on the other hand it extends women's working day, puts their time and energy always at the disposal of other people, limits the possibilities for training or industrial organization and dictates that women's participation in waged work is necessarily discontinuous and intermittent. Indeed it largely structures women's particular position in the labour market, for, by inhibiting their ability to organize industrially, women's double workload leaves their wages to be set simply by competition. But the competition between women in the labour market is not that of workers in equivalent material circumstances. Some women gain a large part of their subsistence through the earnings of the male breadwinner, some are single women with only themselves to support, some must support dependent families solely through their earnings. Inevitably, in the absence of collective industrial organization, the going rate of unskilled women's wages will be set at the lowest level the market will bear – in practice, that sufficient to induce into employment married women requiring a supplementary income. (The value of female labour power, whatever the individual domestic situation, does not include within it the costs of the reproduction of the labour force.)

Many attempts to organize women at work have foundered amid the seemingly inflexible demands of women's domestic life. For the consequence of women's domestic work is not simply a restriction of time and activity; it also shapes women's conception of themselves. The home and its responsibilities persistently invade women's thoughts, fragmenting and diluting their consciousness of themselves as wage workers. A militant worker involved in the Leeds clothing workers' strike in 1970 evoked the effects of women's divided loyalties:

You see, a man's job is to be a breadwinner, isn't it? To earn a wage to keep his family. And he wants what is due to him by hook or by crook . . . Now a woman has a lot more other things to think about. Families and pressures at home, and owt like this. And they cannot be militant enough. If they're militant they're losing . . . Now a woman comes out to work that day; now if she's going to come out to work and strike, well, her home . . . is going to suffer . . . A woman *has* to go out to work, and she works. And a man can stick up for his rights and all stick together, but a woman has a lot more other things on her mind. Feeding her family, you know . . . and you think to yourself . . . [on strike] the first hour you thought to yourself, you're militant, you

31

know, and then by the second hour, you're thinking – 'Oh, I could be doing my washing . . . I could be at home, doing my shopping.' And that's the whole difference.[19]

Men often cite women's lack of militancy as the explanation for their weak representation in the Labour Movement. Mary MacArthur, the founder and organizer of the National Federation of Women Workers in the early twentieth century, acknowledged that women have to be educated into the principles of trade unionism. Indeed, women's divided subjectivity demonstrates that Lenin's idea of the spontaneity of trade-union consciousness cannot be unproblematically extended to women workers. Yet the history of women wage workers shows persistent militancy throughout the nineteenth and twentieth centuries. But it is much more difficult for women to sustain long-term industrial organization. In earlier phases of capitalist development – in the domestic system, for example – production and home coincided and women were often the most prominent in everyday economic struggles. But when work and home are separated, a strategy which depends wholly upon the industrial organization of women is unlikely to succeed in changing the industrial position of women in production. For this is to treat women as though they were men, to ignore domestic work, childcare – women's double workload – and the complexities of social–sexual relations. Feminism is often accused of creating divisions among the working class, but men's and women's material circumstances are different, and so their consciousness of themselves as members of the working class will be different. To ignore this is to overlook the political implications of the social–sexual division of labour. The industrial organization of women in modern industry is a consequence and not a precondition of political consciousness – precisely the obverse of the Leninist formula.

The structural weakness of women's position in industry will

19. Diane Gold, *Leeds Tailoring Workers*, unpublished M S.

not be changed except through an alleviation of their double workload. This can only be accomplished by political and ideological means, through changes in the sexual division in the home and a stronger political presence of women in the state. Marianne Herzog paints a grimly pessimistic picture of women factory workers. They are helpless victims of capitalist exploitation. There is no conscious collective resistance, only occasional solidarity or momentary escape through dreams, though even these are shaped for them by capital, through the words of its pop songs, through its consumer goods. Women's deepest longings remain within the bounds of wage labour: a better-paid job, a small shop. Documentary evidence from other struggles is testimony to the fact that women have been capable of change, of conceiving a vision of a different future, but there are no elements in Marianne Herzog's account of the women, their factory work and their home life which offer a glimpse of how change might occur. The factory totally dominates the lives of the women and the implication is that there is no separate space for the creation of a disruptive politics or culture. Both are unmediated emanations of the rule of capital. This desolate view perhaps underestimates tensions and contradictions in the women's situation, as well as in capitalist production itself. There is no simple logical chain connecting factory, state and culture. Struggle occurs in each of these realms. The past ten years have seen a resurgence of militant feminism. In Britain, equal pay and anti-discrimination legislation and more liberal laws on abortion and contraception are not just paternalistic impositions, they are above all the results of the political organization of women and the feminist presence in the Labour Movement. These are precarious advances, piecemeal reforms, but nevertheless indications that women are voicing their demands, that women are speaking and being listened to. Marianne Herzog's book makes a substantial contribution to that movement.

*

Introduction

The most enduring impression left by *From Hand to Mouth* is its description of modern factory work – not the work performed by an exceptional minority of sweated workers, but the average type of unskilled factory work performed by millions of women workers throughout the advanced capitalist world. This is the importance of Marianne Herzog's book. It lifts the veil from modern industry and reveals the monotony, ill health and debilitation of its working day. It forces us to look at the underside of the glossy commodity spectacle.

September 1978

From Hand to Mouth

We offer you a job for several
months as

Temporary Assistant

working a two-shift system.

We are seeking short-term female workers
for our temporary increase in production
as

Supervisors/Inspectors

to undertake visual supervision. They will,
of course, receive thorough training in their
future work.

If you do not have the necessary experience,
we can offer you a light, mainly sedentary, job
as

Production Line
Worker/Packer

Ring or visit us with your particulars

Staff Department,
1000 Berlin 42, Oberlandstr. 75–84
Telephone (030) 75 08 71, extension 373
Underground: Alt-Tempelhof. Bus: 65, 73

Gillette Deutschland
GmbH

Foreword

In this book I have described work done by women in factories. I have tried not simply to use the words piece-rate and piecework, but to describe what they mean. If we are to fight this kind of work – which becomes no more than a few turns of the wrist – if we are to fight this working-to-the-bone, this having to produce five to twelve items a minute for eight hours at a time, then we also have to describe it. It is important to do this now, when these conditions include the mass sacking of working women. Whenever there is a crisis it is the women pieceworkers who are the first to be thrown out onto the streets. These are women who have worked for years unable to develop their talents, unable to become carpenters or locksmiths, but who have had to put together five to twelve items a minute, who have had to punch, rivet, rabbet or weld, because, in factories, there is no other kind of work made available for them.

In Berlin the big concerns are closing down and sacking workers again after another of the three-to-six-monthly crises. Women who have slaved at piecework are being thrown out before they can get better safeguards against sacking, before their holidays, before Christmas. In their next factory, which will produce an entirely different commodity, they will be faced with the same heavy hours from their training period through the time that they go once again onto the piece-rate. An attempt is now being made to push women down to the lowest grade, to turn them into casual labourers. Gillette, for example, which has sacked 1,500 women in the last two years, is now looking for women who will do shift work for a few months as packers on an assembly line.

Marianne Herzog
Berlin, March 1976

'Bread and Roses'

In January 1912 women and men working in the textile factories of Lawrence, Massachusetts, in the USA, went on strike both against starvation wages ($5.10–$7.55 a week) and against child labour. Undernourished children were forced to work alongside adults, this was a time when children born alive were dying before they reached their first year at a rate of 172 in every 1,000.

The women, many of whom came from Italy, fought particularly hard. They were untrained workers handling automatic machines. They went on the picket-line, were arrested and jailed. When, on 29 January, the police and the military attacked the line, one of the women workers, Anni Lo Pizzo, was shot dead.

The song 'Bread and Roses' came out of the demand inscribed by the women on their banners during the strike: 'We want Bread and Roses too!' and 'Bread and Roses!'

As we come marching, marching, in the beauty of the day,
A million darkened kitchens, a thousand mill lofts grey,
Are touched with all the radiance that a sudden sun discloses,
For the people hear us singing, 'Bread and Roses, Bread and Roses'.

As we come marching, marching, we battle too for men,
For they are women's children and we mother them again.
Our lives shall not be sweated from birth until life closes.
Hearts starve as well as bodies: give us bread, but give us roses.

As we come marching, marching, unnumbered women dead
Go crying through our singing their ancient song of bread.
Small art and love and beauty their drudging spirits knew.
Yes, it is bread that we fight for, but we fight for roses, too.

As we come marching, marching, we bring the Greater Days,
The rising of the women means the rising of the race.
No more the drudge and idler, ten that toil where one reposes,
But a sharing of life's glories, Bread and Roses, Bread and Roses.

Words by James Oppenheim
Music by Martha Coleman

As__ we come march - ing, march - ing, in the beau - ty of the

day, A__ mil - lion dark - ened kitch - ens, a__ thou - sand mill lofts

gray, Are__ touched with all the ra - diance that a sud - den sun dis -

clo - ses, For the peo - ple hear us sing - ing, "Bread and Ros - es, Bread and Ros - es."

My working day (1931)

I enter the factory building. I am hit by the oily air. I am in charge of two looms, 120 cm wide and 100 cm wide. I put oil into the spindles. I set spools on the shuttle spindles and start up the looms. The loom rattles and the shuttle flies. But threads soon begin tearing; I pull out the loom in order to fasten and re-thread, there is a big flaw and I quickly separate it out. The second loom now stops. I put the shuttle in and set the loom going again. I return to the first loom and start that up again. I now put the spools back on again, chase round the beam for any lumps, loops or knots, for that will mean re-fastening threads again if they pull too hard. I return to the looms, which have now both stopped. Take out the shuttles with the empty spools, put in the other shuttle with a full spool again and push the loom back in again. And so it goes on for nine and a half hours![1]

1. From *Mein Arbeitstag – Mein Wochenende. 150 Berichten von Textil-arbeiterinnen* [*My Working Day – My Weekend: 150 Reports from Women Textile Workers*], collected and published by the German Textile Workers' Union, Berlin, 1931

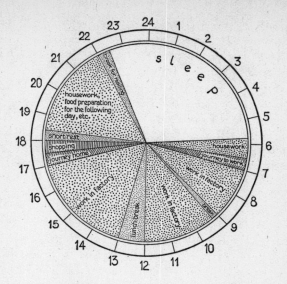

The working day of a woman textile worker

Welding tubes: an eight-hour day

*The first time I went to work in a factory was in 1970, for AEG–
Telefunken. I wanted to find out what factory work was like, what
women workers produce, what they earn. I also had to earn some
money myself.*

AEG–Telefunken has five factories in Berlin, employing 24,000
people. I worked in the tube factory in Sickingen-Strasse. It
employs 2,100 female and 500 male workers and 400 salaried
staff. The women do the productive work, the men are engaged
as specialists. The men, who, unlike the women, are paid by the
hour, are the foremen, the setters, the toolmakers and the
feeders. The women, on piecework, make radio and television
tubes and semi-conductors.

I want to write about these women pieceworkers. In this
factory there is no piecework for men. For two years the
management tried to train first young German and then young
foreign male workers to produce tubes by the piece, but they
had to give the idea up. The women say, 'They were hopeless,
they could never have done piecework.' So the women are there
again as pieceworkers, they have to do it; 70 per cent of all
women in factories are on piecework.

To put it another way: of the ten million working women in
the Federal Republic two thirds constitute an unskilled labour
force. Three and a half million are factory workers and of these
94 per cent are unskilled or semi-skilled. 'Semi-skilled' means
receiving a month's training so as to be able to do piecework,
and, once the training is over, doing the piecework as an unskilled
worker. Only 6 per cent of women factory workers are skilled.

In 1970 there were 30,000 women workers employed in the Berlin electrical industry. It is the branch of industry with the highest number of women workers. Of that 30,000, 29,000 were unskilled and only 1,000 were skilled. It is the unskilled women workers and the unskilled unemployed women who form the reserve army for piecework. They cannot avoid piecework because they will get no other kind.

What is piecework? What does it mean to work by the piece? What does a day's piecework look like? What needs can women workers satisfy despite it, and what forces them to do it?

Division of tube production: Shop 1

There are about 400 women pieceworkers in this shop, which is divided by a broad corridor into left and right. There are 25 rows on each side and each row is made up of 7 to 8 women sitting in front of a machine. The distance between the rows gets smaller and smaller. Every time foremen or engineers walk up and down the women expect the rows to be pushed further together. Conversation can take place over three rows – they are that close. At the same time, more and more foreign workers – Yugoslavs, Turks and Greeks – are placed between the German workers to prevent just that. Over a third of the shop is now staffed by foreign workers, but that is still some way off from half. The machines, which make something between a clicking and a buzzing noise, have a working surface which measures roughly a metre by 65 cm. Around 350 women work at these machines on individual piece-rates; another 30 are on group piecework at the conveyor belt.

There are two conveyor belts, each with fifteen group piece-workers, and it is they who start the construction of the tubes. Each worker in these groups has a box of materials which she keeps between her stomach and the belt, and from which she selects two parts. She fits these into a fixed unit on the moving

belt and presses two buttons. The worker next to her adds two
further parts and again presses two buttons. Selection, fitting
and button-pressing take two seconds. Once it has been round
the belt, the basic construction – the frame of the tube – is
complete. One belt pushes out 10,000 tube frames a day. At the
end of the belt these frames are put into boxes of 30 and passed
on to the individual pieceworkers who, in this shop, continue
with the second part of the production process. The individual
pieceworkers (their job title is 'assembly worker') use electric
spot-welding machines. After the basic construction of the
frames they assemble, weld and check the fine, innermost parts
of the tubes.

On average the worker welds between eight and sixteen spots
on a tube, for which the piecework time allowed is one minute.
The time limits are fixed by the time-and-motion system. The
workers weld tiny bands in the innermost parts of the tube –
that is, they weld contacts together. These tiny contacts could,
of course, be welded automatically and there is a machine
designed for the purpose. But it doesn't do the job as reliably as
the workers because it welds either too tightly or too loosely, or
it produces too much waste. This is largely because the materials
used are constantly changing. The machine puts definite limits
on the attempts of management to use ever poorer material in
order to reduce production costs. Unlike a machine, the pieceworkers can have new ideas every day about how to handle poor
and changing materials. They can weld in different ways or they
can loop the bands round the struts instead of simply welding
them on. In addition, unlike a machine, they can loosen contacts
which have been welded too tightly or they can alter the power
of their spot-welders so that the bands will hold even with the
poorer material.

Apart from the women operatives there are other people on
the shopfloor. There are forewomen whose job it is to supervise
the workers and to enter up their pieces for each day – their place

is at the end of a row. Then there are shop-clerks who work out the workers' wages according to the number of pieces each has produced. They sit alongside the section manager at a large table by the entrance. There are also setters, who adjust the machines, and foremen who set and control the conveyor belt – setters and foremen sit together in a glass cubicle at the end of the shop. While the women operatives are glued to their machines all day long doing their piecework, the forewomen, foremen, setters and section manager buzz round them like hornets.

What are the economic pressures on the women in the shop, and how do they differ?

To understand why women go on with piecework involves an examination of their overall situations. What all the 400 women on the shopfloor have in common is their economic dependence on the factory and that they all experience piecework. Their economic dependence is such that they are forced into piecework for as long as ten to twenty years, though the degree of that dependence differs according to whether or not the women can still change factories. The young ones (and in this shop they are nearly all young), that is the 15 to 17-year-olds and the younger women who are mostly unmarried and without children, can change factories more easily because they are not yet so bound up in a network of ties. It is different for those women whose families depend on the piece wage that they earn and who, because of their age and their children, find it more difficult to move to other factories.

There is a 20-per-cent turnover among the workers in the factory. Those who move are teenagers and young women. A number of the 15 to 17-year-olds come into the factory straight from school, some without having finished 6th or 7th class, yet others having finished only primary school. Some have been in care – that means that they have been released from school only to be living in a home which is itself a kind of school institution. With others it is the reverse: they enter the factory at 15 having left school with the threat of being sent to a home if they don't make it in the factory.

Other young folk come after some kind of training or from broken apprenticeships. One 15-year-old has been working in the shop for three months. She had been an apprentice for a year in a small textile factory where she had not been allowed to use the machines but had been made to spend most of her time there ironing; she had earned DM 140 a month and had been taught nothing. She is no longer interested in another apprenticeship and simply wants to earn money. At Telefunken she earns DM 2.46 an hour.

There is a 16-year-old girl who has been working for a year in the shop. She came to it after breaking off her training as a hairdresser. She says: 'I'm getting on too slowly here. When I'm 18, I'll go into a cigarette factory. Nobody can do the number of pieces required here; every time they raise the wage, they increase the number of pieces.' As a 16-year-old at Tele-funken (in 1970) she earns DM 2.76 an hour. The 15 to 17-year-olds work for time wages; piecework does not begin until they are 18. As they are not on piecework they do not identify with the pieceworkers. They keep their distance and push away the idea of piecework as if it is something that they will never have to do. Because their pay is not tied to the piece, they can frequently get up from their places, run around the shop and the factory, visit those friends of their own age who are working in the same area, and break for a smoke. At first I took this running around as a form of resistance by the youngsters to the lot of the workers who are stuck to their machines. Later I came to realize that it simply constitutes the difference between time-wage and piecework. The attitude of the pieceworkers to the youngsters is contradictory. They know what is in store for them when they come onto piecework. But when a youngster sits next to a pieceworker, the pieceworker too has to keep her distance because she has her piece to do, while the youngster next to her can work slowly and get up a lot.

When piecework arrives for the youngsters, they often react by giving in their notice. Beforehand they are already saying: 'When I'm 18, I'm clearing out of here.' They hope that in a new factory they will get a smaller piece-number, and they will also have another four-week training period before going onto piecework. They can only avoid piecework by leaving again. In AEG–Telefunken the piece-numbers are so high that to begin with the youngsters simply cannot cope. The only ones who can are those under so much economic pressure that they are forced to do this and nothing else. What this means for juvenile and young women workers is that in the years when their economic situation is still flexible they are able to move from factory to factory, until economic pressure finally compels them to stay in one. Economic ties increase when the workers marry, have children, grow old. AEG–Telefunken, like all the other big concerns, will not take on women over the age of 30 to 35. The average age in this factory is 27.

Four women workers who for different reasons cannot change factories

Frau Winterfeld
is 40 and has been doing piecework with AEG–Telefunken for sixteen years. As a 40-year-old she is no longer able to change factories. She is a single working mother and so she must earn more than other women. Frau Winterfeld does regular overtime. She arrives half an hour earlier in the mornings and works half an hour longer in the evenings, she also works on Saturdays. She spends 9 hours 40 minutes a day in the factory. The 40 minutes are for breakfast and lunch breaks – unpaid for workers, women and men. For a 50-hour week Frau Winterfeld earns DM 700–

800 gross a month, but the earnings of a pieceworker are never constant. She has to beat her wages out of the machine each day. It is not enough for her just to be at her machine at 6.30, as a pieceworker she has no legal entitlement, she cannot work a little less one day; as a pieceworker she is paid according to her contract, according to the number of pieces that she produces. If for any reason she should not feel as well as usual, on that day she will not earn, say, DM 4.40 an hour, but DM 4.20. In April Frau Winterfeld's earnings went down by DM 100, for in that month some machine damage meant that there was not enough work and no worker could get overtime. As a pieceworker Frau Winterfeld lives in constant fear of not having a good average, because if she falls ill or goes on holiday, or when Christmas comes, she will not have enough money.

Frau Heinrich
is 33, has been a pieceworker for twelve years with AEG–Telefunken, has a five-year-old son. Her husband works in the same factory and is a shop-steward.

At the age of 33 Frau Heinrich would also find it difficult to change factories. After ten years a pieceworker is considered old. Any new factory she tried to move to would rather take on three young workers and train them, allowing for the possibility that two might leave during the training period and the third stay perhaps only a few years. Frau Heinrich is an old and experienced pieceworker who would settle in quickly, but the new factory would run the risk that after twelve years' piecework she might fall prey to one or even several chronic illnesses, which would mean long periods of absence from the factory. Frau Heinrich knows this too, and in any case she would be no better off anywhere else. During the twelve years she has been able to work herself up to an hourly wage of DM 5. Next to her, in a side compartment of the machine, she has an entire chemist's shop to make this possible – painkillers of varying strengths and

49

different kinds, so that she can get rid of the pain and get on with the work.

Frau Heinrich has been a pieceworker with AEG–Telefunken for twelve years. In this time she has worked on the line, worked shifts, had her child and earned the minimum because she couldn't do piecework then, and has also taken work home for the factory. After getting a nursery place for her child she returned to piecework.

Frau Heinrich hopes some day to become an inspector and so get away from piecework, a hope shared by all the other women. Once a month this hope becomes a reality for her when she helps the forewoman with stocktaking. In the morning of that day she is still plugging away at her piecework, in the afternoon she suddenly gets up, acquires legs and runs around. Otherwise Frau Heinrich never gets up during her eight hours. She goes for her breakfast and lunch breaks five minutes after they have begun and returns to work before they are over. At the end of the day, when the others are wiping down their machines and packing their bags, Frau Heinrich tips out another box of materials onto her machine and welds another 50 bases. She welds 3,140 tube bases a day.

Frau Lange

is 26, her husband is a factory worker. Frau Lange has to work as well. She used to live in the DDR, trained as a telephone operator, but was unable to find any similar work in the West. She married young, round about the time she entered the factory. She has been a pieceworker for Telefunken for eight years. In these eight years she has had her two children. She is still young enough to change factories, but she has spaced her children in such a way that this is no longer possible. Her daughter is five. Frau Lange takes her to the kindergarten in the morning and begins work in the factory a little late. She stops work a little early, fetches the girl from the kindergarten and is back home shortly before her son returns from school. During the school holidays she works on the afternoon shift; she is at home in the mornings and goes to the factory just as her husband is leaving it. In the eight years of piecework she has worked herself up to DM 4.80 an hour. When she has been ten years with AEG–Telefunken she can claim an additional percentage on her pension, which she doesn't want to give up.

Frau Patzke

is 30, her husband is a driver, they have a four-year-old son. Frau Patzke would like another child, and for this reason she will not move. To re-train in another factory and then have a child is no reason for changing; and to leave the workers around her in order to sit among others is also no reason for changing; and in any case she cannot afford to give up the rate of DM 4.80 that she has reached after ten years of piecework for AEG–Telefunken. Frau Patzke works a six-hour day. She arrives at eight in the morning after taking her son to kindergarten and leaves half an hour early to collect him. When she arrives at eight in the morning she is carrying a black shoulder-bag and wearing the white nylon overall that is compulsory for all women workers in the shop; she is wearing cyclamen lipstick. She takes her place next to Frau Heinrich, switches on her machine and puts on a pair of glasses. She only uses glasses for welding – almost all the workers need glasses after several years of piecework. Then she moves her chair so close to the machine that she seems to have crawled right into it. Two hours later Frau Patzke's shoulders are rounded and bent over into the machine. When she leaves after six hours' piecework, her lipstick has gone, her face is tired, sometimes grey, and she looks much older than she did in the morning.

These family and economic ties are why the women carry on with piecework. They are compelled into it because they are untrained workers and have no choice. Piecework is based on these ties, they lay the foundations for the ever-increasing exploitation of women workers through increasingly rationalized methods. And the most economically dependent workers, those who cannot change factories, are those who are the most exploited. Because of the number of years that they have spent doing piecework they can be moved with ease and at short notice to other jobs in the shop. They can do not just one type of welding, but three, four or five, or they can be used on the line or they can spend a morning on inspection.

With some interruptions Frau Winterfeld has been welding the same model for five years. She has managed to get to a rate of DM 4.70. In April 1970 this model is taken away from her and she is given another which she has never welded before and is re-trained for three weeks, during which time she is paid an average of her earnings in the preceding month. After her re-training she is to come onto piecework again. Frau Winterfeld protests by going sick for six weeks. When she returns she is once again put on the new model. After her three weeks' re-training she reaches the initial piecework level and earns DM 3.25 an hour – after sixteen years' piecework at Telefunken. When, at last, she has worked herself up to DM 4 again she is put on yet another model which, though not the same as her old one, is very similar to it. Once more she has to pay for the re-training period, only this time her average is much lower. When, finally, Frau Winterfeld is put back to work on her old model she has learned to weld two new types and has paid for that learning herself.

In this way, after a number of years, pieceworkers are able to weld a number of different models. In the next three years AEG–Telefunken plans to change its production. Semi-conductors are to replace tubes. The living capital for this changeover is the women workers who cannot change their jobs. They will be given re-training periods and learn to produce semi-conductors instead of tubes. After they have been re-trained they will once more have to climb up the piecework scale.

To put up with piecework the women take refuge in dreams in which they can express all their longings. Frau Winterfeld dreams of an ice-cream parlour of which she is the proprietor. She imagines pastries and ice-cream sundaes and invents names for them. Once, when she had a friend working next to her, she told her about her ice-cream parlour and they agreed to share it and to go on dreaming about it together. Frau Lange dreams of the relationships that she had before marriage and how different everything might have been had she married someone different from her husband.

Once a worker said: 'I'd like to go back to school again.' Why she said it she didn't explain, but none of the women was surprised. A conversation about school experiences ensued.

Piecework dreams go back mostly to the past. When they are needed, one fetches them; when the bell goes for a break, they disappear. Immediately after the break there are no dreams, then they are needed again and collected, and while you are dreaming and welding you suddenly come across a familiar spot on the third or the seventh or the tenth tube and you think, 'Ah, here I am again', and then you go back to your dreams until a spot like that comes up once more or a conversation starts in your row or there is a break.

A piecework day

At five minutes to six Frau Winterfeld switches on the light and the current for her machine and for the one next to her. She hangs her bag on a hook on the machine, packs her sandwiches in a side compartment, takes a tin of Nescafé and two cups from the compartment, pours out some coffee powder, runs with the cups through the shop, in her slippers, nylon stockings and nylon overall, opens the door into the washroom, shuts it, runs round the corner, stops at the hot-water boiler. There are women in front of her, holding their thick coffee-pots under the hot water. Next to the boiler some women are standing by the washbasins and looking into the mirrors above them, tidying their hair and putting on lipstick. Frau Winterfeld makes her coffee, turns, goes back through the washroom, opens the door, closes the door, goes along the passageway through the shop and back into her row, puts down a cup for Frau Bartz, who has just arrived, puts down her own cup on her own machine, sits down, pulls her chair up, sets her foot on the pedal, steps on it twice, the machine clicks, Frau Winterfeld takes hold of the first tube and the bell goes in the shop. Of the 400 workers in the section, one third have begun welding.

Underneath her overall Frau Winterfeld is wearing her Sunday dress. As I move along the row to my machine, I hear Frau Bartz asking Frau Winterfeld when she went to bed. 'About two,' says Frau Winterfeld. 'You never learn,' says Frau Bartz. Frau Winterfeld spends the weekend with her daughter at her sister's home and comes straight to the factory from there on the Monday morning. Frau Bartz pushes over to Frau Winterfeld a tube which has some complication she can't handle. Frau Winterfeld says, 'The children didn't get to bed before ten and I couldn't talk to my sister before then.' Frau Bartz opens the drawer in her machine, looks to right and left, sees nobody, takes a bite from an apple and closes the drawer again. 'I got angry with my husband,' she says. 'I sent him out shopping on Saturday because he was sitting around smoking the place out. Then he went onto brandy – well, what do you expect of men, they can't stand being at home. When he came back, everything he'd bought was expensive, it was all the things he liked. Apples for DM 2.20, when you can get them for DM 1.20 – I always buy the 1.20 ones – that's the sort of thing I mean.'

While Frau Winterfeld and Frau Bartz are talking they never once look up, they go on welding, looking at the tubes and chatting. They sit facing the middle of the machine, about a metre apart. Frau Bartz says, 'But I must stop, either I go on chattering or I do my piece, I can't do both.' What she does not say is that she shows inexhaustible patience in helping the women who are training – explaining things to them, adjusting their machines – which means interrupting her own piecework. 'I'll soon quieten down,' says Frau Winterfeld. 'My brother-in-law came home at nine on Saturday. My niece was already in bed and called to him. She asked him where he had been, why he was so late – she even smelled his breath to see whether he'd been at the pub. My brother-in-law came into the kitchen and asked my sister if he should put up with that from his nine-year-old daughter. My sister said, "What do you mean? We all have equal rights in our family, if your daughter thinks you've come home too late she can say so." My nephew was in the kitchen too and he said, "If I told them that at school, they'd think I was having them on." I'll shut up now.'

At 6.30 the bell goes for the start of the general working day. By this time both Frau Bartz and Frau Winterfeld must have welded 30 tubes. By this time about two thirds of all the workers in the shop have begun welding. Frau Heinrich has arrived. She takes out her yoghurt and places it on the machine, starts up the machine and empties onto it the first box of materials. She sits in a row behind Frau Winterfeld and Frau Bartz. Frau Heinrich's work goes in short cycles. You can tell that by the boxes stacked up in front of her which make up her day's task. She almost disappears behind them. Her work-cycle lasts for nine seconds. She picks up a base with her hand and a support with a pair of tweezers and welds the support to the base. She does the same with the second support and puts the finished base in the box. To be able to go on with this Frau Heinrich has extended her movements over the years, within the limits of piecework. She has invented a few additional movements, but still manages to get through the required amount of work. She

55

doesn't simply pick up the materials and weld them together beneath the electrode. If you watch her you see that she spreads out her arms as if she were flying, draws them together and picks up the materials with both hands as if she had come upon them by pure chance. As she does this she rocks backwards and forwards, treads on the foot pedal three or four times, and only then welds the first part. Then out go the arms again. Frau Heinrich uses all this to help her get through her piecework, otherwise it would be superfluous movement and she couldn't afford it. She does exactly the same thing with her feet. She has to weld two spots on every unit, while the other women have to do from twelve to sixteen. But here again Frau Heinrich adds a few movements. While she picks up the pieces and before she puts them under the electrode she treads three or four times on the foot pedal, and only then does the real welding. Frau Heinrich has developed these movements in resistance to the inhuman piecework.

Two and a half hours to go to the first break.

During the first hour the welding is haphazard. With the first and second boxes the unwelded tubes are taken out, welded and put into the grid with the finished tubes.

After the first hour the subdivision of the day and of the piecework begins. The first subdivision is until the first break and it is possible to think of that as the end of the piece day. But even that is too far off for any worker with something inside her head. The time has to be even further subdivided to make it bearable and the work possible. To begin with, the workers divide up the time until the first break into half-hours. Then, depending on the piece, the half-hours are divided into minutes. Some of the women have wrist watches next to their machines, others have alarm clocks. Only those women still in training and the young workers not yet on piecework are able to look at the big electric clocks with large dials placed at either end of the shop. The pieceworkers work by the minute.

Frau Winterfeld divides her half-hours into six periods of five minutes. She has five to six tubes to weld in each five minute period. After one boxful – that is, after 30 tubes – she can take her foot off the pedal for five to seven minutes while she checks her welded tubes under a magnifying glass. When she has checked them all she puts them into the grid with the other finished tubes. She then turns to the next box of unwelded tubes and has again something like a free minute in which to mark all 30 tubes with their number. Having marked the last tube she pulls up her chair again and, with her belly squeezed to the machine, picks out the first marked tube from the new box. She welds the first and then the second part to the tube, turns it round and welds together the fine bands inside, while with the tweezers, which she holds in her right hand all day long, she lays the bands one over the other.

By eight o'clock Frau Winterfeld has welded 120 tubes, four boxes. She still has 60 tubes to weld before the break. She divides these first into two lots of 30, and she has to finish welding the first lot before the music begins at 8.30. Until 8.30 Frau Winterfeld divides the box into three lots of ten tubes, and each ten she then divides again into two lots of five.

At eight o'clock Frau Patzke and Frau Lange arrive.

Frau Patzke sits next to Frau Heinrich in the row behind Frau Winterfeld, Frau Lange sits next to Frau Patzke. Frau Patzke looks attractive, she has a lot of her cyclamen lipstick on, she has taken her son to kindergarten and her husband is out somewhere in his coal truck. Frau Patzke and Frau Heinrich act as agents for Avon Cosmetics. Frau Patzke calls out to Frau Winterfeld, who has ordered cosmetics for her daughter, and passes her a paper bag over Frau Heinrich's machine. Frau Winterfeld interrupts her piecework, takes eye shadow and powder out of the bag, looks at the bill and puts it all in the drawer of her machine; then she shifts up to her machine again and picks up another tube. Frau Patzke notices a portable radio on Frau

Winterfeld's table and asks if it is anyone's birthday. Frau Winterfeld: 'Yes, my daughter's.' Frau Lange says to Frau Patzke: 'Did you read that a whole Telefunken warehouse with a thousand tapes has been burnt down?' Frau Patzke: 'That must have made a lovely fire.'

At 8.30 the music begins.

Until 8.45 Turkish music is played over the loudspeaker, followed by German music until 9. Frau Winterfeld sags. She has been sitting on her chair welding without a break for two and a half hours: 14 welding spots a minute, each one requiring a tread on the pedal; each time she contracts her stomach muscles and each weld produces fumes which she inhales. Her arse hurts, she can't sit on her chair any longer, her calves have stiffened because she can only take her foot away from the pedal every 30 minutes, her left shoulder hurts because she welds with her left hand, she feels as if her spine is broken because she can't lean back.

At 8.45 the bell goes.

A voice from the loudspeaker says: 'We wish every woman a good morning and extend hearty congratulations to all those who have a birthday today. Today we play for you: "Ninette from Avignon", "You Can Only Get It in Carnaby Street" and "Only a Little Glass of Wine".'

'Ninette from Avignon' is over, you could barely hear it anyway. While they slave away the women shout, 'Louder, louder!' The next song booms through the section, 'You Can Get It in Carnaby Street'. It has an mmtata, mmtata rhythm and begins: 'Everything happens in Carnaby Street, a Carnaby boy plays a song on his guitar for the people in Carnaby Street ... yes and everyone finds the one thing that you can only get in Carnaby Street.' It fits in with all the dreams and longings of the women on piecework. It suggests that you only have to go there and everything will be put right, there's no piecework there, no tubes, no fumes. When I began to work in the factory I thought that the songs should be different and I fantasized about what I would play over the loudspeaker. After a while I joined in with Carnaby Street. Frau Winterfeld and Frau Bartz push on. They have no strength left, but they still have their dreams and these help them to weld another ten tubes, another three, another one. Machine off, cup, bread and cigarettes out, and away from the shop.

Fifteen minutes' break. The factory is shaped like a horseshoe. Frau Winterfeld walks with a workmate through the passageways and in two minutes has reached the other side of the factory, opposite her shop – the yard lies in between. She returns and on the way meets Frau Bartz going into the old canteen, she makes another cup of coffee and walks past the washroom back into the shop. Frau Heinrich is in the washroom sitting with three other women on the edge of a row of the kind of washbasins you find on a campsite. Frau Winterfeld puts her coffee onto her machine and approaches a woman in the row in front of her. It's someone she has known for ten years. The woman had emigrated to Australia with her family, but after five years there they returned and since then she has been working again for Telefunken.

Frau Winterfeld returns to her place, switches on her own and Frau Bartz's machine and after the break begins welding again. Frau Heinrich and Frau Bartz arrive too, each with their coffee. Frau Patzke and Frau Lange have carried on working, they don't get a break because they don't begin until eight o'clock. The women say that the time between the first and second breaks is the best. For the first one and a half hours this is true enough because your hands have got used to the tubes. But what follows is too much – slave labour, the women call it. During the break Frau Lange has seen a man, now she describes him to the others. Frau Patzke says, 'Let me have a look at him,' and Frau Lange replies, 'You won't be able to, he's wearing overalls.' Frau Patzke tells how last night at about eleven o'clock she decided to go to bed, but she had to feed the tortoise first.

But there was no tortoise. Frau Patzke was already in her nightdress and spent more than an hour crawling through the flat, arse in the air, until she found the tortoise. She tells this story against herself in such a way that all the women can laugh. One afternoon the previous week when everyone was flagging, someone brought out some photographs of naked women. They passed from machine to machine: 'Wow, some boobs, mine get smaller and smaller, but her arse is just like mine,' and they laughed at each other and at the pictures and could put up with the work for just a bit longer. When the setter arrives to work on the machines, the women fall upon him. 'Oh Müller dear, you look so pinched around the nose, you can't have slept much last night.' Then another woman says, 'Müller dear, you've got such white ears.' He has finished what he came to do and is trying to get away. When he gets to the end of the row another woman calls out to him, 'Müller dear, you've left your overalls behind, is that a hint?' He goes back along the row and says, 'You know I only like 18-year-olds, I've got a woman like you at home.' The woman who teased him is about 30, 'Müller dear' is slightly hunchbacked and limps.

Break from 12 till 12.20.

1 p.m. – two hours to go till the end of the day.

For months the women have been talking about holidays. As early as February Frau Patzke said, 'Thank God I've got my holiday coming up soon, in four months I'll be on my way.' It's May now and the factory shuts down in July. Frau Bartz has already had her holiday in a Telefunken holiday home in the Harz. Frau Winterfeld will be going to the mountains with her daughter, it will be her first holiday in ten years. Frau Patzke and Frau Heinrich, with their husbands and children, want to go together to Romania. Frau Heinrich went there last year, but it will be the first time for Frau Patzke; it will also be the first time that they will go on holiday together. Frau Lange will be staying in Berlin and can look after Frau Patzke's tortoise. Frau

Heinrich talks about Romania: 'I've never seen anything like it. Children can do what they like, no one ever thinks they're in the way, if they're playing then even the waiters carrying heavy trays will move round them. If the children upset anything then waiters come with serviettes to spread over the mess on the table, and nobody will tell children off. My boy is a regular kindergarten child, quite different from one brought up at home. He's learnt how to adapt and to go without things. He starts school in a year, but I'm not worried, the kindergarten will have made it easier for him.'

A few days ago Frau Heinrich began her twelfth year at Telefunken. The foreman passed along the rows just before the factory closed for the weekend and asked her if she was working overtime on Saturday. She just shook her head. He then spoke to a pieceworker in the next row. Frau Heinrich turned round and said to him, 'Today is my twelfth year here.' The foreman went on talking to the other worker; Frau Heinrich said again, 'I've been here twelve years today.' The foreman finished his conversation and, turning to Frau Heinrich, said, 'So you don't come in on Saturdays.' Frau Heinrich shook her head. Shortly afterwards the forewoman arrived and Frau Heinrich said, 'It's my twelfth year here today.' 'My condolences,' she replied.

The machines are ticking away in the shop. Forewomen are running about everywhere, the setters and foremen are sitting in their glass cubicle. Messages are relayed over the loudspeaker, such as: 'A bunch of keys has been handed in, please collect from the Works Committee.' 'Dr Mertens from Oklahoma, please ring 225.' Women are shouting 'Work, work' throughout the shop. These are women who were not given enough materials in the morning to last them through the day, and who cannot move from their machines now to get more because that would mean losing the time to weld five or six more tubes. Frau Heinrich calls out, 'Who'll give me a new back?' Frau Winterfeld says, 'One moment, just one moment,' gets up from her chair, stretches her arms, shakes her head about, shakes her legs and sits down again at her machine.

2.40 p.m. – another half-hour till the end of work.

For Frau Winterfeld it is another hour, but she kids herself and also says, 'Just another half-hour,' and then stays where she is and goes through the whole thing again. Frau Patzke starts packing up, says to a worker behind her, 'Müllerin, what are you cooking tonight?' The forewoman arrives to write down Frau Patzke's piece total; Frau Patzke to her: 'Huh, you foreigner.' When the forewoman has gone Frau Heinrich says, 'The types that wander about here, in a few months they'll be calling us by numbers.' Frau Patzke slings her bag over her shoulder: 'Why doesn't anyone ever look out of the window when I drive off?' Two rows farther on there's a quarrel: 'It's not my job to bring you more work, if you haven't got any, kindly go and get some yourself.' As the foreman walks by, Frau Müller, a single worker with a child, speaks up for a youngster sitting without work: 'What kind of a shitty firm is this where you have to run after work, who's doing the piecework, them or us?' Frau Lange and Frau Heinrich sit at the window and look out at the car park.

After a quarter of an hour Frau Patzke arrives in the car park, she's changed into trousers and is wearing a headscarf. She unlocks her car, an old VW, and nods to the other women. The woman who had been to Australia calls out to Frau Winterfeld, 'What's happening?' Frau Winterfeld answers, 'Frau Patzke is driving off.' The woman from Australia: 'Jesus, I'm nearly there.' The first to leave is Frau Lange who, like Frau Patzke, collects her child from kindergarten. Then Frau Bartz – kindergarten days are over for her, her daughter is 16, the same age as Frau Winterfeld's.

The bell goes at 3.10.

Frau Heinrich packs up. The women on the afternoon shift have arrived. Another woman is sitting next to Frau Winterfeld in Frau Bartz's place. As Frau Heinrich goes, she says, 'If I should ever be born again.' 'Then what?' asks Frau Winterfeld. 'It's obvious, I'd be a man.' Frau Winterfeld's backside still hurts, she can't feel her legs, shoulders, back or belly any more, they've gone numb, turned to stone. She welds with her hands, treads with her feet, checks with her eyes; the forewoman in front of her is making up the schedule for tomorrow. Frau Winterfeld thinks about her daughter, whom she will soon see. Her daughter is an apprentice with Stiller and doesn't get home until after the shops are shut. By then Frau Winterfeld has tidied up, cooked and sat down with a cup of coffee and her first cigarette of the day. Frau Winterfeld says that cigarettes cost too much here – 80 pfennigs each; she means that in the time it takes her to smoke a cigarette she could have welded eight tubes. After nine hours' piecework and 40 minutes' unpaid break, she switches off her machine, meets up with two other women in front of the factory and walks with them to the bus.

Women's work in prison

I was in prison from December 1971 to December 1973. Reason for arrest: suspected membership of a criminal organization. I was kept in detention for two years awaiting trial. I refused to make a statement. I was kept in solitary confinement for sixteen months. I got to know five prisons in four Federal states.

Prisons belong to the state. Prisoners are given a reward for work rather than a wage. Neither women nor men in prison get social insurance or a pension. Just as in the factories, women in prison get no training.

The first thing I hear about women's work in prison are the shouts and orders over the tannoy: 'Get a move on!' and 'Washroom women to work!'

Then I see the names of firms written on the cell doors. The woman shut in behind the door works for the firm either in her cell or in the workroom.

When I take exercise in the yard, I can look for a few moments into a hut where women are making plastic bags.

Prisons I've been in: Anrath near Düsseldorf in Nordrhein–Westfalen. It's a convict prison. One hundred and twenty women imprisoned there are in for life or for long terms. Long terms mean from three to ten years. All the women are convicts and convicts are obliged to work – no training is given. Women are forced to work in the laundry for this and other prisons; they are forced to work in the sewing-room for this and other prisons; they are forced to make up plastic bags in a wooden hut in the yard. They are paid DM 1.50 to DM 1.80 a day for eight hours' work.

Some fifteen women in this prison are lent out to a factory.

Just as in the concentration camps, they are called 'outside detachments'. They leave the prison in the morning under guard, spend eight hours in a local factory working apart from the other working women and men and return in the evening under guard.

Another prison, at Mainz in Rheinland–Pfalz. Ten to fifteen women on remand. There is no workroom. Each prisoner works in the cell in which she is locked up. The work is putting rubber bands through air luggage tags at a set rate which is the required piece number for the day. I spent eight months in this prison. During this time there was no other work for the women. Apart from this I saw women slaving in the laundry, cleaning offices, cleaning the prison, cleaning the medical room: they earned DM 1.50 a day.

In the prison in Hamburg there are 80 women on remand. They work in their cells with a quota: they stick hairpins into cards, they pack tassels in bags, they put together curtain rings, they count fountain pen cartridges into boxes, they wrap up tickets for the State Lottery, they thread strings through bags for cotton wool, they make pan covers.

In the sewing-room they make curtains and bed-linen for the prison and for the staff.

There is no training; they get DM 1.80 a day.

In the gaol in Frankfurt, Hesse, there are 200 women prisoners – juvenile, on remand or serving sentences. They prepare food for this prison and for the men's prison opposite. In the laundry they wash, dry, mangle, sort out and pack linen for this prison and for others. It is heavy work.

In this prison the women sweep, wipe and polish the corridors, hallways, showers, visiting-rooms and offices.

This housework includes cleaning the buckets. There is no drainage in two wings of the prison. Cleaning the buckets means carrying away the shit, washing and disinfecting the buckets. They carry away the dirty water – you get one jug of water for cleaning your teeth, washing yourself, washing your clothes, your sweater and your dishes – and bring back fresh water. This too is heavy work.

In the sewing-room the prison linen gets mended.

In a room for making cardboard cartons, the women fold, rivet, stick, sort and pack various parts of the cartons. Heidi's report on this room follows below.

As in Anrath, women here also go out to work in a local factory. In this case it is the Hammer meat-salad factory. For this they get DM 1.80 a day.

I have read in the newspaper that since 1974 Frankfurt has been providing training for fifteen women as zoo-keepers and florists.

In this prison 180 women sew, wash, polish, change buckets, cook and fold – and these are the facts – for DM 1.80 for an eight-hour day.

Heidi's report from the carton room

Heidi was remanded to await trial in 1973. She reports on her working day in prison. Since I cannot get in touch with her, I ask permission here to reproduce her report.

The working day for Stabernack[1] begins at 7.15 in the morning and ends at 4.45 in the afternoon. At present there are 30 to 35 of us working in the room.

Payment is reckoned on targets prescribed by the factory but which the prison usually increases on its own initiative. Few of the women can reach the target, for which they are paid DM 1.30 a day. If you do more than the target then you are paid the same but you get an achievement prize – this never comes to more than DM 20 a month.

The work can only be done standing up or sitting down. The movements are all the same and you stay in the same place. Many women get back-ache or pain in the shoulders as a result.

We have a breakfast break of fifteen minutes. Most women must choose between eating and smoking a cigarette – there isn't time to do both. For these fifteen minutes two filthy cells are put at our disposal.

After breakfast work goes on until the midday break at 11.30. Ten minutes before this the machines have to be cleaned, which certainly didn't happen to them before they arrived in the prison. The machines come from the Stabernack factories in Offenbach and Lauterbach in an unbelievably filthy and clotted-up state. They are the oldest models which should have been

1. The name of the company for which the women prisoners are working in the prison

properly overhauled and checked before being given to a woman to work at.

We are supposed to take our half-hour exercise from 11.30 to 12, but this is never kept to. By the time we get out ten minutes of the break have gone. We've scarcely been out fifteen minutes before we have to go in again for food. But the women need the full half-hour's exercise because they are working with glue and other adhesives. Sometimes we are not even able to open a window during work because 'the glue will dry too fast with an open window'.

At three in the afternoon we are given ten minutes in which to smoke a cigarette. This time limit is strictly observed. These apart we have no other breaks during work. At 4.30 the women begin cleaning their machines again. The place has to be swept every day. The rule says that the workplace must be left clean.

At the moment we are working for three other companies. The first is called Asbach. For them a woman sits at a riveting machine. Her job is to punch two holes into a folding box. Youngsters will then thread a cord through the two holes and knot the ends on the inside. There are two different targets for this work. For the threading it is 1,500 to 1,800 pieces a day and for the hole-making it is 3,500 a day.

The second company is called BASF. For them we stick and label containers for tapes. Using a glueing machine – an edge-gluer – one woman glues the edges and sides of the boxes while three or four other women sitting at the same table stick them together. For this an all-purpose liquid glue and a thinner are used.

When the boxes have been put together in this way they are taken to a conveyor belt. Here sit on average six women whose job it is to stick plastic bands on the backs of the boxes. Another woman has already cut these bands into the required lengths. She does this standing at the cutting machine and making the same movement with her arm over and over again. She then takes the cut strips to the conveyor belt. Two glue rollers are attached to the front of the belt and the strips are passed through them. When one of the women working at the belt has stuck strips on twenty of the boxes she takes them to a table where another woman sits inserting slides into the strips; these slides have first to be folded. Once all these processes have been completed, my job is to take the finished boxes and wrap them in packing paper in batches of 20.

The women who stick the strips on the boxes are supposed to produce 3,000 a day, that is, 500 a day for each individual woman. No one, so far, has achieved that, the average is 300 to 400 per woman.

The whole process produces 1,500 to 2,000 items a day.

The third lot of work comes from a company called Döhler. Once again this is glueing folding boxes. Stabernack has provided an extra conveyor belt, kept in the packing room, specially for this work. It involves seven women. Two stand at glueing machines, one stands at the conveyor belt and the others sit at the tables. The pre-punched boxes are first folded by five women. This is done sitting down, but it is such monotonous work. All the women have bandaged hands, they have been rubbed raw by the surfaces. The women have been doing this folding work for weeks now. They can't even raise their arms properly, they hurt so much. If you say anything, the answer is, 'Yes, we know how tough it is.'

The women at the glueing machines glue the folding boxes on the inside – an all-purpose glue is used for this too. These women also have a container of thinner beside their machines. This is used not only in the glueing process but also for cleaning the machines at midday and in the evening. The room where these women work has, at most, one open window. All the women complain of headache and sickness; the air inside is unbearable. If a match were struck, everything would go up in flames. Many women have to leave their work to be sick in the lavatory. Supplies of thinner and glue are kept in canisters in a cell, but the open canisters are left standing in the workroom during working hours. In the evening they are put in a glass cabinet in the front workroom. Many women can't come back to work after the midday break because they can't stand the fumes. Yet they are still expected to produce 300 pieces a day. That has never been achieved either, the average is 200 a day, which, of course, is not enough for 'them'.

Whatever the work, the target has always been set too high, so that the women have never been able to reach it. If the women complain about the targets they are told that they would be higher outside. Most of the women lose any desire to work once an impossible target has been set.

Loading and unloading trailer trucks is also much too hard. The heavy cartons have to be carried from the truck to the back entrance up three steps – the drivers do the minimum possible. Loading and unloading always seems to need five women and they are simply borrowed from the workplace, but no allowance is made to them for their time away. So by the evening they are down on their time and piece totals, but no attention is paid to this. If a woman does several hours of loading and unloading she is entitled to a bigger merit bonus, but this is rarely given.

The most important things that need changing are:

a. A longer breakfast break.

b. Half an hour's exercise and enough time to eat afterwards.

c. Something should be done about the glue and the thinner. They cannot be tolerated for any length of time and are a danger to health. The way these things are stored should be changed.

d. We should have a say in how high the production targets are set. Given the working conditions that exist at present – including the bad old machines – we cannot possibly reach the required targets. Either the targets should be much lower or they should be scrapped altogether.

Skilled – unskilled

After prison I had to earn money once more, and in theory I had two possibilities.

The first was to go back to my profession. In 1957 I had completed my apprenticeship as a bookseller in the DDR. I basically liked the work because during my apprenticeship I had had some good experiences – I mean daily conversations with the kind of people who would never enter a bookshop in the Federal Republic. I enjoyed stacking up our delivery vehicles with books, visiting schoolchildren in the villages, visiting agricultural cooperatives or soldiers: people, that is, with few books at their disposal. Or spending hours with the director of a young people's work centre looking out books for the youngsters. Before looking out the books the director would tell me about the youngsters.

But when I thought again about going back to my profession after leaving prison, I realized that both bookshops and academic libraries were out. In an academic library I would have only catalogue numbers and index cards to deal with, and in the years I had spent in the book trade in the Federal Republic I had experienced nothing that would make me want to return. I think this was because I was selling books to people who already had so many compared to those whose working and living conditions didn't allow them access to books.

There only remained the possibility of working in one of the many City lending libraries, lending out books to women, men and children from the locality. I knew that the clientele of City lending libraries was different from that of bookshops. I wanted to know whether I would be able to advise young people or adults in their choice of books, whether conversation was possible, whether I would be taken on.

When I tried, it turned out that there were long waiting lists for these posts, but I had to earn money immediately.

The second possibility was to take unskilled work, and I wanted to try a factory. I did not want to be an unskilled child-minder, an unskilled salesgirl in a department store or an unskilled orderly in a hospital. I didn't want to be a waitress or a cleaner. There just isn't much else. And if I have to do unskilled work in a factory, then I want to go back into the metal industry.

Packing spare parts for lorries

Munich, August 1974, during the economic crisis. There are no vacancies for women advertised in the papers. I go to the Labour Exchange, look at the list for industrial women workers and find just three vacancies. Two months later there were no more there either. Of the three vacant jobs I take the one with the highest pay, DM 6.30 for heavy work.

I don't remember much any more. I mean that I don't remember as much as I used to about my working experience. I say that because as I write this report what I remember best is how little we had in Munich. What concerned me most at the time was how to get the money for the next meal or how to get an advance for the next week. During that time in Munich I didn't feel like writing about my working conditions - I did write, but irregularly, in little bits and pieces, usually after I had done everything else.

Writing a report on working conditions is also an economic question. You need money for the rent and money for food in order to sit at a desk and write things down and write them well.

What I wanted was physical work. It's an old longing which I've never been able to satisfy fully. I've spent time at Telefunken sitting doing individual piecework, I've worked on the production line in a chocolate factory, I've done group piecework in a big printing shop, and again individual piecework in an electrical factory. Each time the piecework chained me to the machine as it did all the other women. I couldn't even walk around. I've never been able to find work in a factory where I've been able to move about.

The firm I went to in Munich was called Bayerisches Verpackungsunternehmen (Bavarian Packing Enterprises). It employed over a hundred workers. There was no works committee. The firm packed exclusively for MAN (Maschinenfabrik Augsburg–Nürnberg). Domestic orders for spare parts for lorries manufactured by MAN were packed by women and men working at the factory, but orders from the armed forces and from abroad were passed to this company. Close by was the goods station of Milbertshofen.

In the morning I set off on my bicycle from the north of Schwabing, up Schleissheimerstrasse, past the BMW works, over the Petuel ring-road, and then I rattle along a cobbled pavement. I lean the bike against the shed and enter the building. Inside it is filthy, old, high and with potholes in the concrete floor. It is approximately 100 metres long and 30 metres wide. Carpenters work near the entrance and we, the women and men packers, work at the back. If you want to speak you have to shout over the noise of the circular saws. It's cold and there's a draught all day long from the entrance which is only shut at night. We never get outside and have no sun, and we aren't properly inside because there is no door to protect us from the weather. The women say that in the winter you can see your own breath. The building stinks of the exhaust fumes from the fork-lift trucks. The air is thick with the dust from the circular saws, the dust from the wood shavings and glass wool used in the packing, the dust raised by the sweeping of all this muck, which is done with a broad broom of the kind used in railway stations.

To cope with all this filth and with the work the men begin boozing at eight o'clock – the women a little later. The carpenters make huge wooden shipping crates and special boxes for bulky or particularly heavy individual parts. Into these massive crates or special boxes we pack all the spare parts for the lorries, everything from a gasket to a radiator. A crate of spare parts weighs about 400 to 600 kilos and is carried out of the building by fork-lift trucks.

When we go from the building into the yard it's like coming up from underground into daylight. We are covered in dirt, oil and sweat and after half an hour's work your snot is black. The railway leading to the goods depot runs right by the factory entrance and goods trucks stop just outside. Sometimes I see a woman with a pram: Yugoslavs working there, women and men, live with their children in huts on the firm's premises. I can't spend long outside otherwise the woman with whom I work has to do more. Back into the factory and back to the potholes, the muck and the packing table.

This goes on from Monday to Friday. Friday is pay day. Every week everyone goes to get their pay. From hand to mouth – the money from last week just lasts to Friday and not a day longer.

We are completely broke. On the Friday of the first week I collect my first advance, DM 100. At Penny's I buy bread, butter, rice, noodles, coffee, smoked ham, liver sausage, tomatoes, two pieces of meat and green beans and pay DM 41.11. We have DM 58 to last the weekend and the whole of next week up to Friday. By Sunday noon we are down to DM 20 for the whole week. We haven't been to the cinema, we don't need fare money, yesterday we just went out for a beer. I don't know where else it went. I buy the food and Ruth pays the rent, gas and bills. At first there were just two of us in the flat, then when Adriane moved in there were three, but that hasn't improved our financial situation very much. Ruth and Adriane both work at Siemens.

I remember my first week, when I was trained by the oldest woman there. She stood behind the packing table, which was approximately six metres long, and I stood opposite her at the other end. I learned about the spare parts, I learned their weights, I learned when we should use wood shavings for packing and when we should use glass wool and where they were both kept. The old woman taught me how to put a bale together and how to line an overseas crate with paper. She showed me where the pallets were kept and how to get them to the table. I learned how to drop heavy spare parts into a crate lined with wood shavings – I learned that after catching a finger because I didn't let go soon enough. I learned that oily spare parts are packed in oil paper, dry parts in thick wrapping paper, and that some parts are not packed in anything at all. I learned which parts can simply be put in as they are and which have to be packed in layers. I got the tool I needed for this from the stores.

After the first week I was allotted my own table along with Frau Schuster. All the other tables had a man and a woman working at them. Frau Schuster had been there a few weeks longer than I. Before that she had worked for eight years on the line in a Munich printing firm. She had been sacked with other women and was then out of work. She got this job, as I did, through the Labour Exchange. First we discussed our wages and discovered that I got 20 pfennigs an hour more than she did. At the first opportunity she demanded that we should be paid the same. When she started Frau Schuster worked at the other end of the yard in the department that dealt with the orders from the armed forces. It was a women's department made up of German and Yugoslav workers who were unable to go anywhere else. They were also unable to move from their workplace, received an hourly wage of DM 5.80, and had to fight a foreman who tried to stop them from smoking.

Schuster and I tried to develop a rhythm together so that we could do what we wanted – get breaks and whatever else would do us good.

What was it like there? Did it offer more leeway than short-cycle piecework? What is 'heavy work' – what is heavy? In that factory I didn't weld contacts together with an electrode, I didn't use tweezers. We got an order which could be anything from four to twenty pages long, each page full of descriptions of the various parts. When we couldn't find a lift-truck driver we put the necessary spare parts in metal cases and took them to our packing table on a trolley, and we did the same with the wooden crates. If we were packing in pallets then I climbed into the crate. If there was no man available or it was too silly to go on hollering for one, I hammered the nails in myself. This fixed the crate to a wooden base. Then we fetched armfuls of wood shavings and glass wool. Everybody worked standing up except the person calling out the checklist of spare parts, who sat on a metal crate. Even this exception only applied when the job involved the packing of small parts. When Schuster was calling out the parts she also had to collect them from a metal crate and carry them to the packing table. I did the packing and then carried the packed items to the big wooden crate. Not only did these parts weigh anything from ten to thirty kilos, but they were also cumbersome. It was all very tough.

If there was something that I couldn't manage, then I'd ask Otto. He was 74, had once had a small shop and had never paid his stamp, so he had no pension and still had to work. He packed like an artist and I watched him working in the crates as often as I could. 'If only I knew why I like you,' Otto asked in Bavarian.

Overalls were provided but no other working clothes, so after the first month I had shredded one pair of jeans and two pairs of shoes. You lost sandal straps and the soles of normal shoes wore out at an incredible rate. There was no dust-extraction equipment and no extra allowance for dirt. In the canteen you could get cold sausage, cheese and beer but no warm food. The dirt in the building and the exhaust fumes from the fork-lift trucks gave us sore throats every day. After a few weeks Schuster said, 'Christ, I'm going to start drinking.'

At eleven o'clock we had our first beer and for the first time for two hours the sore throats were gone. The men began drinking three hours earlier and got through eight to ten bottles a day. One of them, an older worker, was subsequently dismissed for drinking. This man used to do occasional carpentry repairs for a couple of women where he lived, and they paid him in fresh sausage which they got free from the meat factory where they worked. One day he offered me some of the sausage and then went on providing me with it every day. The sausage was kept in the canteen refrigerator in two identical packets, and he used to mark mine with a number. I ate it with bread rolls that I bought from the baker on my way to work.

I hadn't written anything for weeks, when I experienced my first industrial accident. At least, I experienced it as an accident but that is not how it appears in the statistics. In the morning on my way to work I saw a slogan with a coloured picture of a fork-lift truck painted on the wall of a house. It read: 'Get Fork-lift Trucks Out of the Factory.' A few hours later in the packing-shed a fork-lift truck driver dropped seven three-metre wooden beams and fifteen bales of paper onto the workplace of the old woman. Suddenly she was not there, not in the place where she normally spent eight hours packing. I was so angry at the way everyone simply went on packing. The factory management had not kept its promise to stop any further loading of material over working space, which is in any case forbidden. This accident occurred just three weeks after a fork-lift truck had run over the foot of a member of the management. A week later Stephan, the carpenter, lost two fingers in the circular saw, and on the same day the inspector of electrical equipment discovered on his annual check-up that the lamps over our heads were not properly earthed.

Days don't exist any more – days, nights and weeks are all jumbled together. When I leave the factory at 4.15 p.m. I can't believe that I entered it at 6.45 in the morning. It doesn't feel like a day, not like eight and three quarter hours. The pace is such that I know in my bones and in my head that it is not an eight-hour day. I used to feel exactly the same at AEG–Telefunken, where I also knew in my bones and in my head that I had worked for ten or eleven hours – but try proving that out of an eight-and-three-quarter-hour day of women's factory work. I feel that ten or eleven hours with the last breath I take before a break, with the last breath before the bell goes. The end of the working day comes when all your energy, all you are capable of down to the last ounce, has been extracted from you – for the day. Then, as I cycle down Schleissheimerstrasse, I try to find new energy: I want to live. While I'm riding I perform arm exercises for the pains in my shoulders; they don't help much.

I had wondered whether 'heavy work' was easier to cope with than short-cycle piecework. The one does me in as much as the other. With both I need hours to recover and to find fresh energy. But what is heavy work like during the working day? I have feet and I can run around, and because of this I can see other people during my working time. I can carry news between workers who cannot leave their machines. I can get myself a few minutes of sun and air in the yard. If I feel like making a complaint or defending myself, I'm soon on my feet without having to worry about stopping my piecework. When I fetch a crate from the carpenter I can speak. When I'm squatting in the yard measuring crates or writing things on them, if I want to I can talk to passing women and men workers. That is the difference.

At 4.45 p.m. I am at the place where I sleep, at 6.15 a.m. I leave here on my bike. As I climb the stairs to our flat, I think, 'Wage Labour and Capital'[1] and would read the book immediately if I had it. I can have a moan when I get into the kitchen, or I can ask for my back to be massaged. I can decide to eat first or to have a bath. But when Frau Schuster gets home she is faced with three children. She's not allowed to moan, the children want everything from her all over again. She hasn't got a bath, so the first thing she does is put her feet in a basin of water.

There's a note in the kitchen saying where my food is and

1. By Karl Marx

79

giving me the day's news. 'Saw the ear specialist today, he really confused me, said my hearing was normal. If you come to pick me up leave at 10.30. Take Belgradstrasse down to Knorrstrasse and then on to the Frankfurt Ring. It's a straight journey all the way. Ruth.'

Ruth is on the late shift at Siemens this week and when I leave in the morning she is still asleep. When she gets back from her shift at around midnight, I am already asleep, but I wake up and as Ruth talks and eats I slowly become wakeful. Ruth gets tired and falls asleep but I stay awake until about two. The alarm goes off at 5.30. All the statistics get it wrong, it's not just people on shiftwork who work shifts but all those connected with them too. The children of shiftworkers live by shift rhythm.

Meeting people off the late shift is pleasant in the summer. I dawdle along on my bike and make sure I arrive too early. There's a stretch of grass in front of the works where I can lie down. The lights are still on in the upper floor of the factory, the bell hasn't rung yet. The women I am meeting have been assembling and soldering electrical relays. They weld, solder and assemble 3,500 of them a day, every day. Sitting next to me on the grass are Yugoslav women who are meeting friends, sisters and sisters-in-law. We chat, eat cherries, smoke – we belong together. The men, who have come to fetch their wives, sit in their cars or stand by them in the car park in front of the grass. They have arrived too early as well. When the factory lights go out some of the men start up their engines. A little later we hear the approaching women talking and laughing, and as they come through the last gate they pass us in groups which are more like knots slowly disentangling themselves.

MAN sends an inspector. Otto and Maria are missing 600 metres of tubing which they are supposed to pack. MAN says that they have been delivered. I remember packing several crates of tubing two days ago, but I didn't count the metres. That day

1a and b. Women working in the metal industry then and now

2a and b. Women working in chocolate production then and now

3a and b. Piecework

4a. 'When I talk to Jedina I have to stop working . . . I think: I'd like to describe what it means to do piecework, I'd like to be able to tell other people what women's piecework is.'

4b. Marianne's dream: 'I see myself at a machine in a shoe factory. We have developed shoes to suit everybody's needs . . . We know how to do everything.'

5. 'What do pieceworkers get at the end of the day? They have either completed or not completed their piece-number . . .
The next day they are faced with the same piecework, the same piece-number.'

6. Woman welding (1941)

7. Women strikers at the Pierburg factory

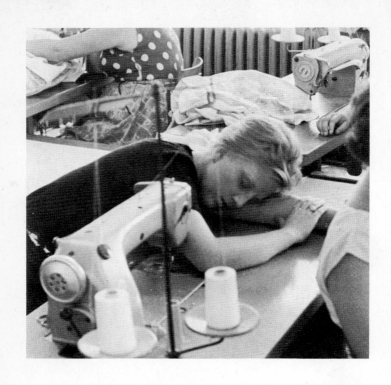

8. 'Everybody's goal is the next break.'

Schuster and I had a good time. We'd discovered by chance that we were both at the World Festival Games in Berlin in 1951 and we talked about it. I went there as a Young Pioneer[2] and Schuster went with friends who had told her about the games. She told me the story. They had travelled in several groups and at the Bavarian border with the DDR they were asked where they were going. Schuster told the officials that they were going to the World Festival Games in Berlin. They were forced to leave the train and were interrogated for several hours. They were asked where the invitation had come from and if they were members of the Freie Deutsche Jugend.[3] Some of the group went back, but Schuster dug her heels in and was finally allowed to travel on with the others the following day. The MAN inspector has a pointed beard and white fingers and looking at him I think, 'You won't find anything.' Even if I really have packed too much. He upsets us all. Willi, who weighs, seals and stamps the crates, has to wrench them open again while the inspector rummages. Otto and Maria are interrupted as well, even though they have a big order from Abu Dhabi, worth DM 400,000, to fill in three days. This deadline has been set by management, who hover round us smelling of scent whenever there's something to be done fast. There is a boom in September 1974; orders have been increasing for a year. They come from Cyprus, Turkey, Greece, Israel, India and Abu Dhabi.

And the wages? Otto, after nine years as a packer with this firm, gets DM 8.50 an hour. Maria, after eight years as a packer, gets DM 6.80 an hour. Schuster and I are both earning DM 6.30 an hour.

After two months I get gastritis, am registered sick and in fourteen days get the sack. They give two reasons. First: 'We

2. The Communist Party's organization for children. In Eastern Europe most children are expected to join

3. Free German Youth, a Communist organization in East Germany for young people from their early teens on

didn't know when you would be back.' Second: 'Someone saw you on a bicycle.' It's October 1974 and I'm sacked while I'm ill. When I go to pick up my wages and cards they say they would like to re-employ me. In this company they like to employ and train new workers because it is never the firm which provides the training but always the other workers, who have to work harder as a result.

I meet Frau Schuster in the wages office. She had developed a foot ailment after I had fallen ill and has also got the sack. We go together to the nearest pub, and we agree that I will look out for work for both of us and will ring her every evening.

The old woman at the third packing table is standing right in the middle of all the filth. For herself and her work she needs pencils, chalk, spectacles, cigarettes, a lighter and a bottle-opener, and she keeps all these things in a cardboard box on the table. Her husband died two years ago after 25 years of marriage. I can hear and see that she works even harder now. She stops on Thursday evenings when we still have a day to go, but only if there is no foreman to persuade her to come in the next day because of rush orders. She has Fridays off because she starts work every day earlier than we do. Once, in the middle of the week – she had been working over the weekend like the rest of us – she laid her head on the table, completely exhausted, and fell asleep. She didn't hear the bell which rings once in the middle of the break and again at the end. We woke her then. She refused to be driven home, got back on her feet and went on working. She is proud. I have heard her express her hatred for Hitler, during whose régime she refused to have children and so is childless. And I heard her murderous call for the death penalty.

Shortly before the last bell Schuster and I massage each other's shoulders. She is so tough that I have no effect on her. After that we take off our overalls in a small windowless room, a cell. The flowered plastic curtains over the door don't draw properly and the men peer through. Sometimes we even fall over the chair that stands there, the room is so small. Then there are another two or three minutes to the bell. The clocking-in box is on the other side of the partition where we change. Schuster goes off through the yard while I get my bicycle. I catch up with her at the gates and walk with her to her bus stop. At the weekend she puts my overalls in her washing machine.

Packing olives

I am packing black and green olives and fat, fleshy pepperonis.

I am no longer packing shipping crates, no longer packing spare parts for lorries. I don't need wood shavings, glass wool or a measuring rod.

I am in Munich in a factory which is five rooms in a cellar. It is owned by a Greek man and there are no machines. Tables and chairs come from a second-hand dealer, there are rusty household scales and plastic shovels. Twenty women sit at the tables, twelve from Yugoslavia and eight Germans, and two men work in the store-room.

I didn't seek out this job, I simply couldn't find any factory work in the autumn of 1974. The pay here, DM 5.25 an hour, is a starvation wage. Only Siemens offers less, paying its women packers a starting wage of DM 5.11.

I rang Frau Schuster, but with three children to feed what could she do with DM 5.25 an hour?

We pack olives for the retail trade. 100 grammes, pounds and half-pounds go into thick plastic bags, are filled with water and sealed. By the evening my right hand is burning as if it were on fire. The pepperonis are kept in salt water and we put our hands in it all day long without gloves. The firm takes on employees without giving them a work contract or asking for a health certificate. The paint is peeling off the walls. If the pepperonis fall onto the dirty cement floor, we pick them up again and pop them into the delicatessen bags.

Smoking is forbidden and we eat olives while we are packing. The olives gleam as if the sun were shining on them down here. I often abandon the shovel and use my hands, letting handfuls ripple into the thick plastic bags. They jostle each other as they roll in and I find the black olives even more beautiful than the green. I place each bag on the scales, throwing in more olives until the weight is right, then I knock the bottom of the bag against the table's edge to make room for the salt water and the sealing. The water is added by the next worker, who also seals the bag.

That's how it goes, I think to myself, a few decrepit rooms in a cellar, decrepit chairs and tables and a cheap workforce, women.

The Greek has put out the same advertisement for years, it reads:

PERMANENT WORK.

Good pay for capable women

Semi-sedentary work for six to eight hours daily.

The older woman who works next to me has been here for four years and earns D M 6 an hour. At 2 p.m. all the German women pack up and go home, but I remain, the only German with all the Yugoslavs, until four o'clock, that is, for eight hours. The women who leave at two o'clock all have husbands who earn money. On my second day there, after the first hour of the morning, I am called out by the Greek and given the sack. On the first day I had talked with the other women about starvation wages.

'You are a Communist,' the Greek says to me. I say nothing. I have nothing to say to him, I am just there for the hourly wage. He stands before me trembling, holding more than the agreed wages in his hand. He is afraid. I take the banknote from his fingers, go back in and say goodbye to the other women. Out in the street I buy two large pieces of smoked bacon from the butcher opposite and walk slowly back to our flat.

I look for work

It is the first of October 1974 and I am at the Labour Exchange. Only the cowardice of the interviewers stops them from pulling our mouths open and tearing out our teeth. 'Are you German?' 'How old are you?' 'What can you do?' After the interrogation comes the answer: 'We have no work at all in the metal industry.'

I leave and look in other rooms for two women who were working in the Labour Exchange a few months back and who understood what work was. At one time one had worked on a fruit farm and the other had been a production worker. They were both on the side of working women and against the money-makers. I discover that they have both been sacked.

The following morning I leave the house with a plastic carrier containing my newspaper and sandwiches and, because I am unfamiliar with the city, a map. I leave determined to find work today, and with the feeling that I will. In the underground I think of men who have been sacked and who still reach for the handles of their briefcases at the same hour every morning as if to go to work, but who have no work and will not admit it.

Two factories are advertising work in today's newspaper; they are Enna and Luitpold. When I ring the Enna works they refuse to tell me what the hourly rates are, they treat them as secrets. But the hourly wage is the only reason women have for working in the factory.

Luitpold, however, does give the information. The employment clerk tells me that the starting wage is D M 6.80. That is a rare wage for a woman; I imagine that the work must be ghastly.

Clerk: What have you done up till now?

Self: In my last job I packed spare parts for lorries.

Clerk: What we need is someone with a pharmacist's or a nurse's basic training.

Self: You mean that you only take on pharmacists or nurses as unskilled workers?

Clerk: It's a matter of precision for us, you see.

Self: For an hourly wage of DM 6.80?

Clerk: Yes.

Self: What are the hours?

Clerk: From 7.15 a.m. to 4 p.m.

Self: Shifts?

Clerk: None.

Self: Well, what's the work?

Clerk: It involves the preparation of organs. More precisely, peeling off the fat from frozen animals, but we've got enough women for that now. We want women to sterilize and drain ampoules.

Self: Is that conveyor-belt work?

Clerk: No.

Self: How is it done?

Clerk: You work in a small room.

Self: With how many others?

Clerk: Alone or in pairs.

Self: I don't want to work alone or in pairs.

Asking after your basic skills, as in this telephone conversation, is not unusual. In the present crisis factories and labour exchanges demand qualifications for which they themselves have never provided training. Because no other work is available anywhere else I go along to Luitpold's factory. Perhaps they'll be taking on women for the animal organs. What they say on the telephone is haphazard and changes from week to week. That you soon discover if you ring up every week.

It is a new pharmaceutical factory situated in the south of the city. Next to the main factory is a new building. A fat porter sits outside and, as in every other factory, you are given a pass. In the employment office they give me a questionnaire. I had forgotten about the questions they ask on these things and wasn't ready to make up the answers. 'Where have you worked up till now?' 'Where does your husband work?' 'How many children have you got?' 'Have you ever been dismissed and if so why?' 'Do you have any convictions?' 'Are you pregnant?'

'I'll take this and fill it in at home,' I say. 'But it may be just what you want,' says the employment clerk, rushing up and taking the form out of my hand. 'What are you afraid of then?' I ask.

It is after 1 p.m., where will I get work today? I count my money – DM 3.80 – and find the nearest telephone box so that I can call the employment departments of the big factories.

Siemens in the north are not taking on any more labour but Siemens in the south are. The starting wage, in October 1974, for both shift and piecework is DM 5.11 an hour. Rodenstock are not taking on but quote their starting wage, DM 5.50 an hour. BMW are not taking anyone on and refuse to give information about their starting wage. Reemtsma are not taking anyone on and will give no indication of what they pay. Pfanni-Werke are not taking on, but when they do it will be for shiftwork at DM 5.55 an hour. They say that they are not taking anyone on until Christmas and that they do not pay for holidays. Until Christmas the women there have to do the work of two, and are threatened with those who have been sacked from other places and are waiting jobless at the door.

At the end of the day I telephone Frau Schuster and say, 'I haven't found anything.' 'Take it easy,' she says to me, 'nothing'll turn up before Christmas.'

Excursion home

I am on an express train to Waren/Müritz in Mecklenburg, in the DDR. It is sunny autumn weather. I see elderberry bushes, rowan trees and wide countryside. I left Waren eighteen years ago and I try to imagine what I looked like as an apprentice. I put on my glasses in order not to miss anything. Then upland with birches and tall, extremely slender pines. 10.40 a.m. I see an eyot in the river with birches, reeds even. Apple trees are laden with fruit. Opposite me in the carriage he reads the sports page and she a novel. You can't lower the windows any more, there are dormer windows which push open. Borgsdorf – Lehnitz – Oranienburg – Löwenberg. Cows are black and white, brown and white. There are potato fields, brick houses. Not a single multi-storey building. 11.15, Dannenwalde, the first lake. Fürstenberg, with sandy soil and pines. 11.30, Düsterförde – Prewin – Strelitz-Alt – Neustrelitz. Twelve noon, Kratzeburg and two lakes. Klockow – Kargow – Waren/Müritz.

In the toilet I hear again, after such a long time, the cleaning women speaking Low German. Where shall I go first? Left into the town or straight ahead, the quickest way to Müritz? (Müritz is the largest lake in the DDR.) I finally decide to turn right to Westsiedlung where I grew up. The long, straight road to Siedlung is dusty, Mecklenburg-ish. You don't get dust like that in Berlin, but that I knew already.

I also know the cobbled paving, but I did not know that there would be corn growing between the cobblestones. The length of the road in front of me is more or less how I imagined it, but not the width. I have always had a powerful image of this road,

89

very long, broad and rising slightly. But now what I see is just a village road.

I pass the Station Hotel and in front of me is the Sun Hotel. Shall I do it or not? I cross the street, enter a block of flats and look at the names on the letter-boxes. But the name I am looking for is not there any more. He was a middle-distance runner and I was a hurdler. Next must come the baker's where black bread is 51 pfennigs. We bought black bread from this baker at 51 pfennigs for thirteen years.

I have reached the end of the long street and the proportions are all wrong again. Here is the corner which I found so difficult to go round as a child. This was mostly because of the wind, and I can still feel it on my belly, but sometimes also because of the slippery ice. Now the corner curves so gently, it is so harmless, a simple corner with no problems.

Round the corner I should be able to see the housing estate and the block of flats where we lived, but I see something quite different. The whole of Friedrich Engels Square, including the sandpit, is now built up. It is now the Friedrich Engels School. In my memory the block where we lived was big, cold and austere; seeing it now, it looks round and countrified. The unfenced front gardens have a comfortable feel. Knitting things, children's toys, a chair, a child's wheelbarrow are among the flowers. I open the door and in one stride I reach the wooden banisters; another stride takes me up several stairs and I find myself – though I would have liked more space between me and it – in front of our door. As we don't live there any more I can't go in any more. I see from the letter-box that the old Caspars still live in the flats. I walk round the block. In the yard there are rabbit-hutches, hens, strips of cultivated ground and stacks of wood. I'd like to sit down and have a beer. There is a state shop across the square. That's where I'd like to go, but it's shut. I squat on the stone steps in front of the shops and light my first cigarette since I've been here.

I want to go to the water, I want to see Müritz. I go once more to the corner but instead of turning in the direction of the station I cross the main road. If I followed the main road I'd arrive in Klink where my aunt lives, but I haven't time for that today. On the other side of the main road I walk down a gently sloping path. When I used to go down it on my scooter I would ride standing, circling the trees and avoiding the tree-roots.

There it is, Müritz, as flat as a pancake and as large as I had imagined it. The surface of the water is still and smooth, but ten minutes later it may be rough. It produces waves, and drowns people every year. I can see to the bottom. It has light-coloured sand shaped by the waves and the currents, just in the way that asparagus beds are formed, only more delicately. If I tread on it or touch it, the white sand disintegrates into dust.

I spend the next few minutes thinking and wondering if I should come back to live here. I'm definitely drawn to it. I look around: there's a holiday family at the other end of the beach, otherwise it's empty. I go to the kiosk in search of beer, but it's shut – by September the summer season is over here. Upturned tables and chairs lie in front of the kiosk and I set up a table and put a chair beside it and look at Müritz from a distance. It's beginning to glitter now.

A fisherman arrives speaking Low German and complaining when he finds the kiosk shut. He had knocked off work specially early to get here in time to get a schnapps and a beer. I ask him what he is fishing for and he says eels. I ask him where they go and he says Rostock. He smokes one of mine and I smoke one of his. I tell him that I come from Berlin and that I used to live here, grew up in Westsiedlung. He says he still lives there. I say goodbye to him, there's a lot more I want to see.

I could set off on an excursion round the shores of Müritz, but it would take days. I walk on until I reach the path by which I came, but then instead of taking the main road I turn sharp right along the Gerhart-Hauptmann-Allee. The Allee runs along beside Müritz and by it I make my way back into the town. At the crossroads at the end of the Allee I have to make a decision. I decide to take the road to the bookshop.

This is the bookshop in which I did my apprenticeship. I began at the age of fifteen and stopped after my examination at seventeen. As an apprentice the bookshop seemed to me to be bigger than the town, and in a way that was true. We were a district bookshop and ordered books for outlying shops, we had the largest turnover and the most extensive list. Standing once again in front of the shop I see that it has doubled in size. A few buildings farther on there used to be a private bookshop, now it is the second state bookshop. I just look into the windows. I don't want to speak to anyone today, I just want to see things and I haven't very much time. The handwriting on the shop door giving the opening times looks like Anne's. She came for a job one day during my apprenticeship and stayed on. She had trouble with the books to begin with, but she had to serve the customers and if she could not find a book or was supposed to recommend one I would pass the titles to her from behind.

Opposite the bookshop there used to be an old café with brown wooden chairs and marble-topped tables. I had to go there several times a day with a tray to fetch coffee. Now it is an ice-cream parlour. I go in and everyone that I see there is eating the same portion out of identical glasses. Out and down to the end of Lange Strasse; there is Schauburg, a cinema. The cinema is being renovated, which is why the showcases are empty. Back into town, the other side now, and I turn off the main street into a side street and come to water again, to the Tiefwarensee. Then I come to the only café. As a child I used to go crazy over the chocolate éclairs in the window, so in I go, through a swing door, between tables and chairs to the cakestand. There are fruit flans and thick, tall fancy cakes, but no éclairs. Out and past the shoe shop, across Friedenstrasse and into the Museum of Local History – entrance fee 50 pfennigs.

The formation of the landscape interests me more now than when we visited the museum from school. Next come the Stone, Bronze and Iron Ages. Upstairs under 'Anti-Fascist Struggle' I see *Der Stempelbruder* [*Brother on the Dole*], the February 1933 issue. It begins, 'Comrade on the dole - comrade worker', and in the text they are fighting against the introduction of industrial conscription. And I, standing at the glass case, am unemployed.

On the ground floor I look at the birds of Mecklenburg and this alone makes the visit worth while. Behind the museum there is a garden with live animals. I suddenly find myself by a pool at the end of the garden, and looking at it more closely I know that I once fell into it. A few buildings farther on from the museum is a school office where my mother worked as a typist, and the pool borders on that building. I stank when they pulled me out of the ice.

I must hurry, my train leaves at 5 p.m. I've been hungry for some time. I find myself at the corner of Friedens-Ecke Freundschaftstrasse [Peace and Friendship Street], and I go past the prison. Don't you know it, don't you recognize it? As children we used to climb up the hill behind the prison and look down into the prison yard. I used to see men behind barred windows and men sawing wood in the yard.

It's another five minutes from here to the station. At a tobacconist's shop I buy something for Ruth which I'd have liked myself. On my right is the road to the station, and I have another thirty minutes before the train goes. There is a Mitropa restaurant[1] in the station and I read the menu on the door. I see wild boar and venison goulash. I find a seat and order wild boar. 'It's off,' says the waiter. 'What is there today?' I ask. 'Egg and potato salad,' says the waiter. 'Anything else?' I ask. 'Nothing else,' he says. 'I'll have that then.'

1. This is the name of the state organization which runs all railway catering facilities

Siemens is taking on workers!

Ruth and I and a Turk are sitting on a corner bench. We are sitting wedged between injured workers, women and men. We are sitting in Siemens in Berlin. In front of us the swing door to the medical room slams to and opens. To our right people are called to the doctor by number, always four at a time.

After ten minutes I am dog-tired from the numbing silence, from the noise of the door. The women aren't sitting here for free, they won't achieve their piece-number today, I know that. It takes about fifteen minutes to leave the machine, go downstairs to the medical room, have a new dressing put on or swallow some pills and go back. That time is not paid for.

I light our last cigarette. The Turk notices that we have only one and gives Ruth one of his filter cigarettes.

It's 8.30 a.m. We got up at 6, the cards from the Labour Exchange say 'Appointment 7.30 a.m.'. The door next to the medical room has no handle, to get out we would have to ring the bell. This handle-less door now opens. 'New employees,' shouts a man.

Now it all begins. You are given a red form by the reception clerks and you fill it in at tables and chairs that look like the counters in a post office. You get up and hand in the form and then you are given a book to read from. The letters are tiny, any normal person would use a magnifying glass. If you don't pass the sight test, if you can't read the tiny letters fast enough, then you are out. We are still in. Now put the right hand then the left hand round an appliance and grip. Siemens is measuring the sweat on your hands. The result is expressed in figures which are stamped on our documents.

94

We are given application forms to fill in and sit down with them at the tables. After ten minutes I hand mine in and am sent back – dashes won't do. I must say whether I have had any convictions or whether I have ever been threatened with any. Whether I have any physical injuries or disabilities. I say no. If they could, I believe that they would breed people even more exploitable than those they have now, people without heads, just with the organs needed by Siemens for production.

The clerk stares at my completed application form. He opens a steel filing cabinet and looks under the letter H. Ruth has finished, and comes up to the counter, both clerks examine her application form and establish that she has worked for Siemens in Munich. They check the sweat on her hands again. I am given a pass for the personnel department. Ruth is given another form: which branch of Siemens did she work for in Munich? What work did she do there? Who was the foreman and which shop was it? 'Be quick,' I say to Ruth, nudging her, 'I'll wait for you in the street.' I'd prefer to take her with me now.

Outside in the street the ground is frozen, there is a thin layer of ice where there were puddles yesterday. I am hungry. Nobody is about and I wait, it seems endlessly, for Ruth. When she comes she tells me that the clerks want to make inquiries with Siemens in Munich and then write to her. We wonder what we should say to that. Our aim is to be in a factory together – what do we do now? We decide that I should go ahead, we need the money.

We walk some of the way together to the personnel office. It is ten minutes' walk, passing the Siemens buildings: first the manufacturing section, then administration. On the way Ruth goes into a pub, she is cold. I meet the personnel manager and receive a lecture at a small conference table. I would be joining a new department; it would be very clean and orderly there. 'There's one thing we can't be doing with,' he says. 'If you go sick, the firm has nothing more to do with you.' A grimace: 'Of course, we can all fall ill. A private question – are you pregnant?'

95

'Bastard,' I think to myself, and ask what the hourly rate is. 'As you come from the metal industry, DM 5.25 an hour.' He is lying, it doesn't matter where you've been, the starting wage at Siemens in January 1975 for all women workers is DM 5.25. No, I haven't a tape recorder to take down my conversation with this dealer in human beings. We're looking for work, that's why we're here. A forewoman from the department I'm supposed to work in comes into the room during this conversation and sits down at the conference table. I'm still asking about money: do they pay fares? 'No,' he says, at first taking me to mean (or pretending to) reimbursement for my ticket today. 'You earn more doing piecework,' he says, and the forewoman nods. 'Piecework, piecework, tell me what that is then.' Forewoman: 'The foreman will show you the work now.'

In the shop the foremen and setters stand around as if nothing ever happened here. A foreman takes me around but I don't pay any attention to what he says. I don't recognize anything in any case – no single whole part, only tiny contacts. The women look up, but they look more at what I'm wearing than at my face. I stop by each woman and start counting. I count at five successive machines and at each one repeat the count several times. With four of the women I count to six and in one case to nine. On these jobs the process takes from six to nine seconds – this is why the women are so young here. I see Turks and Germans, none of whom can be over 25.

I hear the foreman say that the work done here is for news broadcasting. I look around me some more. Everything is new in this building; with the naked eye I can't detect a single fault. This must be a pilot development. Something new is being tried out here: in new premises, with new machinery and with particularly young girls. A woman who has been doing piecework for ten years is not in a position to cope with six-second work units. That means ten parts a minute – a hundred parts in ten minutes.

The shop clerks and setters are not in glass cubicles here as they are in other factories. They sit at desks on a platform along-side the workers. I feel that I'm in gaol, in a new and modern one that I've never seen before – I've got to know the old ones. Does the comparison only mean something to me because I've experienced prison? What difference is there between this new building without a blemish, this working-to-the-second with new machines and even magnifying glasses, and a newly built prison – a Köln-Ossendorf or a Frankfurt-Preungesheim? In neither is your life your own. Connections are snapped into fragments, healthy faculties and organs are destroyed.

On the way back I meet Ruth coming towards me, she couldn't wait that long in the pub. We pass a department store and I suggest that she quickly gets a copy made of my employment form, which I have kept all the time in a folder.

Who would believe it? It's January 1975 and piecework, shiftwork, for one of the biggest companies, brings in an hourly wage – after six weeks – of DM 5.31. I still have to go for a medical check. Ruth waits in the cold. I already know I won't go and work there, but I'm thinking that if there's nothing else and we have no money I shall have to.

What follows is the examination and this you have to have experienced. This I find the most difficult thing of all to describe. Why exactly is that?

At Agfa in Munich I would not say when my last period was, or whether I was pregnant, so I was presumed to be so and not employed. I am too bound up in it to say whether it is the questions themselves which make me lose my temper.

'Is there any mental illness in your family?' the doctor asks. 'Any tuberculosis?' 'Have you had any serious operations?' 'Is there cancer in your family?' You blow into an apparatus, have your teeth examined with a pocket torch – it's a slave market. In the War, I imagine they checked that you had a pair of shins before they enlisted you.

From Hand to Mouth

'Do you suffer from phlebitis?' 'Do you have gastritis?' 'Do you have circulation problems?' His questions indicate what the major illnesses are among working women. Siemens wants to finish you off by itself; it will not employ a woman made ill or worn out by AEG or any other company. The eye test is long and thorough – not for the eyes, not for the workers – the point is: do you see well enough for Siemens? Do you see well enough to produce tiny component parts on piecework? Are your heart and circulation still good enough for piecework? Piecework paid in Berlin in January 1975 at a rate of DM 5.31 an hour.

Assembling a vacuum cleaner:
an eight–hour day

Work makes life sweet, sweet as machine oil.
I spend all day making things I don't want to make at all.

Ton Steine Scherben[1]

It was the only factory looking for women fitters, and they
wanted several. Otherwise there were two small firms, each of
which wanted one woman. We did not want to be separated, we
wanted to work together, and anyway we preferred not to be in
some dump of a small firm. As we drank our coffee Ruth and I
looked at the job advertisements. We didn't know the factory
and only discovered what they produced when we got there.
When we were taken on and they asked when we would start,
we told them that it would be two days later.

The factory

Electrolux in Berlin has a labour force of 600. Its main works is
in Sweden and it produces household equipment. The factory
is in Tempelhof.[2] Gillette is opposite and there is a chemical
factory next door.

You pass the gate-keeper and the clocking-in box and you
come to a concrete yard from which you can go in several direc-
tions. Lorries are parked and components for production are
stacked in the widest part of the yard. If you turn to the right
you come to the section where skilled workers are employed in
the specialized production of deep freezes. If you turn to the left
you come to the women engaged in mass production.

1. A German rock group   2. A district in West Berlin

From Hand to Mouth

The first thing that strikes you as you enter the shop is the turmoil and noise. Gradually, through all the noise and the heat – even though it is summer the windows are shut – you begin to pick out the working women. We are German, Turkish, Yugoslav and Greek. I cannot describe the shop in detail to you because I haven't been taken round it myself. Like every other woman working here I was simply put straight into the place where I am now sitting. My place is in the front part of the shop, which gets narrower towards the middle.

Over there is the lift for heavy loads and the glass cubicle where the foreman and a shop clerk sit. I have scarcely spoken to women working at the other end of the shop. I never get down there and I am not even sure what they do. All I know is that roughly eighty women and ten men work here making vacuum cleaners. You can easily see that most of the women work separately, but there are two groups on collective piecework. One of these works at the noisiest machine in the building. A male worker puts pieces of sheet metal into it which come out as square containers, the casings for the cleaners. The women operate a machine which covers these with a plastic skin. The women and men in the second group punch, rivet and glue the covered casings. The women working individually assemble, drill, weld and stick together the component parts which have been manufactured by women working for other branches of the company in Sweden and England or for sub-contractors in Germany.

What we have assembled is picked up by the women who work at the carousels. These are wheels with ten slots from each of which a vacuum cleaner is suspended. At each carousel stand two women, turning it and fitting more parts, including the motor, to each cleaner, and this is the hardest work in the building. From here the completed vacuum cleaners go on a conveyor belt to be checked. The women not only have to fit the parts together but also have to carry them across the shop to their workplaces, and the motors and cases are very heavy. Walking round the place might be a good thing to be able to do, but with our piece-times it only causes stress. One hundred and seventy vacuum cleaners is the quota for two women in a day. After the rate-fixer's visit to the shop in the summer of 1975 this was increased to 190.

Training period: What is a semi-skilled worker?

Work begins at 6.30 a.m. and I am given half an hour's training by a woman who is a deaf mute. She pronounces words in a way that I can't understand, but makes up for it by showing everything to me so clearly. By seven o'clock I am already sitting at an individual workplace. The half-hour of training has turned me into a semi-skilled worker able to occupy this place, and my job for the next four weeks consists of getting onto piecework. The starting wage (called Wage Group 1) is DM 5.65 an hour and lasts for the four-week 'training period'. I can't live on it, no one can. After that I'll go onto piecework and then get paid piece-wages. I shall have to assemble 480 pieces a day, which means 60 pieces an hour, one a minute. By 10.30 I'm in a nightmare: I take fright when a woman talks to me, I hear the machines whispering, I see travel-bags on wheels even though they are only metal cases. I light a cigarette and think, this is how it always is; I experience this condition whenever I work in a factory, it's the monotony which causes it.

By 11.30 on my first working day both my palms are shredded by a sharp part I have to fit. I am still a trainee and not yet on piecework, but the women who need my parts are. They hang about me constantly waiting for fitted parts because there are none in reserve. I feel hassled, my hands tremble and I forget the sequence of parts. It's worse after the lunch-break when I'm about to begin again – then I have a complete blank about what I've done in the morning.

I feel like an old woman when I leave the factory – not, God knows, like someone who has only been there for one day. In the street Ruth asks, 'What have we earned today?' 'Between us about DM 8o,' I say.

The training period is no less tough than piecework and getting onto piecework is no less tough than staying on it. That doesn't mean that we learn anything during the 'training'. 'Semi-skilled' means 'unskilled', a semi-skilled woman remains an unskilled woman. The training period just means the time in which you learn to work fast enough to get onto piecework, and if you can't do it then you can go. More politely they say, 'We regret that we find it necessary to part from you.' In the Federal Republic the training period for unskilled working women is anything from fourteen days to two months and during this time a basic wage is paid. For women this is always below DM 6.

The piece-number remains the same from the first day that you slave at it. In the summer your fingers may swell with the heat so that the fitting, welding and punching slow down, but that will not alter the piece-number. If you have a period and so are not able to work so fast, or if your children are ill, then that's your problem! Each woman must thrash out of her machine the required piece-number over and over again, every day.

The boredom. At first I can't look up from my work at all because I keep on forgetting the sequence. This is because it has no meaning, it bears no resemblance to anything else that happens in your life. When at last I am able to look up, I scarcely ever do so because of the demands of the piece-number. I keep my eyes on the metal plate I am assembling, which is my biggest part. I see my work place: it is a filthy hole piled up with boxes – full of materials or scrap, boxes full of completed lids. There is one box for each worker for her coffee, handkerchiefs, pills, bread and newspaper. In the middle of all this is a swivel-chair and a female worker. Below us is a cement floor, above us neon lighting.

Behind me sits Jedina. When a long and tedious period has passed and I am suddenly aware of seeing nothing but metal plates, I turn to her and ask what she is thinking or what she cooked last night. If she has cooked, I ask so many questions that I know every vegetable she used. At first Jedina looked on me as a competitor – she had been ill and I had arrived while she was away. I think she stopped competing when she realized that she worked faster than I did, and that I would ask her about things when I wasn't sure. Or maybe she stopped when I quite simply asked, 'Jedina, can you do twenty pieces for me please?' Unlike me, Jedina works for time wages because she is a 'float', that is, a worker who is moved from place to place as need arises. She became a 'float' after working for five years in this factory. Her husband lost his life in an accident here in Germany and her two children, aged eight and ten, live with her mother in Yugoslavia.

When I talk to Jedina I have to stop working, but she carries on. When she gets up and comes over to me I carry on. As I sit there assembling parts, drilling, putting away the assembled lids, I think: 'I'd like to be able to describe what it means to do piecework, I'd like to be able to tell other people what women's piecework is.'

Piece-number: 1

6.20 a.m. In order to spread the load a bit, many women, including me, arrive a little earlier. We have clocked in and hung up our coats and jackets in metal lockers just like those in a barracks or a prison. The women walk through the building shaking hands, the machines have not started yet and it is almost peaceful. Some women are looking at their newspapers, others are standing in groups talking.

6.30 a.m. I line up my swivel chair with my work surface. Jedina gives me her hand while looking in another direction, as she does every morning, and passes on. I light a cigarette and call out 'Good morning' to the woman on the other side of the belt, who is already working. The gangway is immediately to my left and beyond it Sylvia and Sonya work with others on group piecework. Renate is there too. Being a float, she is put somewhere different every day.

I start on my first 60 pieces. One part that I put together goes into a crate with several layers, each of them holding 60 parts. So I count not by the individual piece but by the layer; I have to complete one layer in every hour. A piece means putting five parts into each lid that Erica has assembled before me, and for this I use talc once and drill three times.

An older worker, Alma, who sits on the other side of the materials belt from me has an even higher piece-number than I have, and smaller parts to assemble. She used to work at two machines, but now a single machine has been built to take their place which demands a proportionately higher piece-number. The new machine gives her more work to do, but because she is no longer able to change machines she can't move about so much. Alma looks like a goldsmith or a watch-mender when she is working. She has made a very special and fine tool for herself, looking like a pair of tweezers, which she uses to insert a tiny part into a spool. The movement of her hand always looks as if it could never be repeated, as if she were not doing piecework but constructing something very special, which, of course, is what she could do, what all the 'unskilled' women sitting here could be doing.

It is 7.30 a.m. and I've done 50 pieces. I should have done 60. Erika, who works behind Jedina, puts a new box on top of the lid which I still have to assemble, so blocking the view ahead of me. She always does this even though she knows how much it annoys me. I jump up and push the box onto the floor and am able to see again. Erika just stands there and says, 'I feel terrible today.' This 'feeling terrible' is an inarticulate, dumb cry. You hear it several times a day in the factory. Everyone knows what it means, but it is never clearly expressed, it is never given a name. To break that dumbness and to bring out what is meant, you need time. 'Good,' I say, 'don't bring me so much.' I get up to go to the lavatory and immediately feel better. After all I have done too few pieces this morning. I walk down the gangway, past the individual work-benches, past the glass cubicle where the foreman and the shop-clerk sit – they don't have a piece-number, I think to myself – to the empty lavatory. There is muck on the floor, two washbasins for eighty women, no toilet paper, no soap, no hand towel. Twice a week women come from a cleaning agency to tidy up. I leave quickly, go back the same way, adjust the position of my chair and get on with my piece quota.

Everyone's goal is the next break. It is 8 a.m. All the machines are running, it's very noisy. There's no point in trying to talk to Jedina now, we can't understand one another even if we shout our heads off. I sometimes bellow a sentence to Sonya and Sylvia. If we want to say more we have to interrupt our piece-work and go over to one another, something that happens at most three times a day and then only very briefly. By now I should have produced 90 pieces in ninety minutes' work, but I've only done 75. If you fall behind in the morning it's almost impossible to catch up, because the afternoon piece-number is the hardest to get through. I move closer to the machine. Each time I finish a lid I put it away and take another out of the box. Jedina, on the other hand, stacks ten or twelve finished lids in front of her where there is already a heap of materials. She can't see anything in front of her, but she only takes two to three minutes over a box of 20 pieces.

I push a lid over a gadget on my work surface. With my right hand I take hold of the first plastic part and hold it steady while I place the second against it with my left hand. Then I take the metal plate in my left hand – carefully, so as not to cut my palm to pieces. With my right hand I take a rubber ring and fit it onto the plate. Using a finger I rub talc onto the inner side of the rubber ring and stick a rubber stopper into a drill hole. I then slam the metal plate onto the lid – often it won't fit properly. I take the drill in my right hand, pick up three screws with my left, exert pressure and secure the screws. I miss out on the checking in order to catch up with my piece-number. I put the finished lid away with the others and carry on knocking up piece totals.

Sonya from over the way appears next to me. 'The rate-fixer is downstairs, he'll be up here next week.' 'Let's talk in the break,' I say, and go on working. Sonya goes. It's 8.30 and another half hour till the break. Furious that I have no time to talk to Sonya now, I spoil two pieces, have to drill them open again and so lose yet more time.

You may ask why I don't chuck in piecework. There are three reasons. The first is that a basic time wage allows you to pay the rent but not to have a good meal. Second, if you don't produce the set number of pieces for a basic wage you're sacked. Third, a newcomer who chucks in her piecework makes something to joke about and no more – and rightly so.

I whistle against the noise. I can hear Jedina's drill more clearly than my own – sometimes we drill in competition without mentioning it. It's another fifteen minutes to the break. I don't want to do nothing but drive myself from one break to the next. I saw a play at the weekend, *Summer Folk* by Maxim Gorky. It's a mammoth play. All the most important roles are women's and by the end of the play everyone can see that the actresses are dropping. They are weak and their knees are shaking from their efforts as they come onto the stage again and again for the applause.

What do pieceworkers get at the end of the day? They have either completed or not completed their piece-number and they have earned from DM 6 to DM 8. The next day they are faced

with the same piecework, the same piece-number. 'Enough!'
I tell myself. I pour Nescafé and tea into two cups and queue
up at the hot-water boiler. The Germans get themselves tea or
coffee in cups, the Turks and Yugoslavs have it in cans that
several of them can drink from. The woman who is last in the
queue shouts, 'Hurry, hurry!' She does it every morning, it is
the same inarticulate cry as 'I feel terrible today.'

Piece-number: 2

I didn't talk to Sonya about the rate-fixer at break-time. As
soon as it began she came over and asked me what was in the
newspaper and we discussed the front page instead. Then I
walked about the building for a bit. I found women talking to
each other and, as on every other day, I saw women with their
eyes shut, resting their heads on their work-benches for a few
minutes.

One woman frightens me out of my concentration on the
piecework. She comes along the gangway and says 'Good morning'. I feel under attack. I've been here for an eternity and she
says 'Good morning'! I look at the clock and it's 9.45. She
starts work at this time every day, so she has the right to say it – I
calm down. When your physical exhaustion is greatest, when your
last holiday, your last day off, even your last break, was too long
ago, when the weekend wasn't long enough for you to recover –
my last weekend wasn't even long enough to let me get over my
bad temper – when all your energy is gone by Tuesday, then you
feel the super-exploitation of high piece quotas so keenly that
you think your hair will turn white. So when a day comes in
which, because of some failure in supply, the women in a particular section have only half the normal work to do you really
feel the difference. On such a day I will assemble not 480 but,
say, 280 pieces. This has happened only a few times, but we have
felt so much better on the way home when it did. Our heads were

not so hacked about by the piece-number and the minute-by-minute rhythm. The damage that piecework does to the head – where has that ever been expressed? Why do I find it so hard?

What can I still see of our daily struggle to live? I can describe laughing women workers, or I can see an old male worker massaging the shoulders of a woman pieceworker who has stopped working for a moment. I can see Sylvia's eighteenth birthday, which we spent all day in the factory celebrating. I see how much we deceive, lie and notch up piece-numbers which we do not achieve – but how little we are able to get away with it! I see the old woman who shows us her breast because she has something that she wants to tell us about it. I see, too, how we care for one another, bring along bargains and find out what sizes of clothes and shoes fit those we are fondest of. I know how we discuss children's schoolwork, or marriage breakdowns, or how one woman has run away to another man because she can't stand it at home any more.

The period after the first break from 9.15 till the midday break at 12.30 is the worst marathon. In front of me I have my first 60 pieces. I need to complete another 195 before the midday break, then another 135 in the afternoon, which together with the 150 I completed before the morning break will make up my total of 480 pieces.

I look over to Sonya and Sylvia. Sonya is sitting at the riveting machine. She is 24 and has a child, but Sylvia still lives with her parents. Sonya puts the riveted tins on the floor and Sylvia builds a wall with them. Sometimes they build towers and sometimes pyramids or whatever else occurs to them each day. A few minutes later the wall is so high that I can no longer see them. I get up and go over, they are both squatting behind the wall of tins and smoking. 'I prefer your other model,' I say, and hear them shout, 'We don't.'

Eleven o'clock. At this hour I always have the genuine feeling that eight hours have passed. Everybody goes on working, but I should like to buy myself out, put a note on the table and scram for the day. Once I allowed myself this luxury. It was while I was working for MAN in Munich packing lorry parts, and I was tired out. There were three of us in the flat, two on shiftwork, and I got woken up when they came in from the late shift around midnight. One Friday the men in my shop were drunk and swerving around on fork-lift trucks. I thought that if I didn't go then I would either create an accident or get involved in one. I could still stop a crankshaft rather than get it on my foot. I told them what I was going to do and at twelve I was gone, unpaid and redeemed. It felt like a luxury. The sun was shining outside and I was on my bicycle, riding down the cycle track on Schliess-heimerstrasse. I imagined what Ruth and Adriane would say when I turned up during my working hours. I went faster to make sure of seeing them before their shift began, promptly lost my balance because of a heavy plastic bag I had swinging on my handlebars, and landed on the bonnet of a parked Volkswagen. I bruised my shin and bent my bicycle, which I then had to straighten out. A woman passed by, hobbling along just like me, and told me that I shouldn't go on riding. But I told her I had to and got back onto the bike. Back at home I collapsed with laughter telling Ruth how stupid I looked perched on the car with a painful shin. Ruth had never seen me like this before and left the kitchen. I cooled my leg with a flannel and laughed even more because I had a free day. Ruth showed me a clothes stand she had made that morning, I touched it and it collapsed. Ruth and Adriane left for their shift and I picked up the bits and pieces.

11.45 a.m. The belt next to me won't carry the boxes any more and they are knocking against one another. The noise is unbearable and you can't take it for long. I see the setter in the gangway next to the belt move off in the opposite direction. I shout after him and then get up and shift the boxes on the belt myself so as to put a stop to the noise. The women sitting next to the belt do this several times a day, having to stop their piecework to do the setter's job for him. He is a big, heavy character in grey overalls who is so bored that he doesn't know what to do with himself. He will sometimes sit for hours opposite a pieceworker watching the woman slave away. In desperation he has already lit himself two cigarettes at once.

I am in my place again holding the drill in my right hand. I glance over at the first carousel where two women, one Turkish and one Greek, are working. The Turkish woman is working so fast my eyes can hardly follow her. She is taking foam rubber rings out of boxes, slinging ten of them over her left arm; they are white and large and look like giant bangles. She runs back to the carousel with them and puts one on each of the ten vacuum cleaner motors hanging from the carousel, running round it and turning it as she does so. I drill in the screws, check that the switch works, pick up the next lid, look up and see that the Turkish woman is now running round the carousel attaching plastic hoods which she carries ten at a time, stacked one and a half metres high on her left arm. With her right hand she pulls them apart and attaches them.

I can also see the second carousel with two Yugoslav women working at it. Paula is just off to fetch a new lot of motors. She stacks them dangerously high on her trolley. Then she bends down, lowering her head to give herself more strength – pictures of slaves behind trucks come to mind – and pushes the trolley back to the carousel. Paula stacks up so many motors on her trolley in order to save the extra minutes that would be lost in a second journey. If someone knocks against this dangerous load from the front then Paula will get one or more of the motors on her unprotected feet. All the pieceworkers collect motors in this way, and as long as there's no accident and as long as the women get through their piecework, the foremen turn a blind eye.

Someone is giving me a shove. An older woman who works a long way behind both me and Jedina is holding a bag of sweets under my nose. I am so startled out of my solitary world that I can't recognize a single sweet. I take a dark one. 'Take more,' she says, 'they are so small.' I take a red raspberry one and two green ones. As she goes I feel that I would have liked to say more to her. I see Alma putting her hand into the bag and making a careful choice. It's another three quarters of an hour to break, another 50 pieces. I jump up. Past the first carousel, round the corner, past the fourth and fifth, Ruth is fitting parts at the sixth. I put the raspberry sweet and a green one on the carousel and give her a quick squeeze of the shoulders. She is just as startled as I was and says, 'Where did you get them from?'

I hate the piecework I am doing here more than ever. In AEG-Telefunken we also sat separately, but we were so close together that at least we could speak now and again without having to shout. In this factory the individual benches are too far apart for you to speak to one another. However, the main point is that in the Federal Republic factory work for women is restricted to unskilled work and it stays unskilled. Ninety per cent of it is piecework with work-units of under a minute on average. This has a ruinous effect on the brain and body of every woman worker. This unskilled labour, this piecework, is still classified as light work. 'Unskilled' is equated with 'light' and slotted into the lowest wage groups, the light wage groups. There is no provision in the factories for giving unskilled women workers any kind of further training. Of the three and a half million women working in factories in the Federal Republic, 94 per cent are unskilled and only six per cent skilled.

I am aware of a constantly recurring thought inside my head and I have to keep pushing it aside in order to go on with my piece-number. For the last half an hour I have been telling myself to get up and go and see the foreman. A boy who had been taken on at the same starting wage as the rest of us wound up with DM 100 more on his wage-slip even though he was in the same tax bracket as the rest of us. As I think about it I reach for the next unfitted lid and then throw it back as I realize that

From Hand to Mouth

I am just going on working – it is very difficult to break away from piecework, from your piece-number. As I walk down the gangway I've forgotten about piecework, I'm only interested in my wages. I push open the door of the glass cubicle and talk to the foreman. When I've finished, he looks at me and says, 'That's equal entitlement, I can't do anything about that.'

I decide to go to the wages office, but when? Women have to go to the wages office every day, official certificates are only obtainable there and those who work in the wages office never come to the women who work on the shop floor. Pieceworkers have to interrupt their work, but they are not paid for the time it takes to walk from one end of the factory to the other in order to get to the wages office. Back in their places again, they rush to make up the loss on their piece-number. In theory it is the job of the shop-clerk who sits beside the foreman to telephone the office for the workers, but this one does not represent the interests of the women, even though she is the only woman on the works committee. The women prefer to go to the office themselves.

Piece-number: 3

1 p.m. The last round. It's like being in the ring here, except that the rules are much harsher. Another two and a quarter hours till the end of the eight-hour day, another 135 minutes, another 135 lids to fit. I am alone with the afternoon's piece-number – and the backlog from the morning. I see pictures which I have never seen before. I see myself at a machine in a shoe factory. We have developed shoes to suit everybody's needs. We make sandals, shoes and boots and provide a pair of each for every adult and child every year. I can also see Sylvia, Ruth and Sonya in the shoe factory. We know how to do everything: we know how to maintain, repair and improve the machines; we know how to produce good shoes and how to take part in production discus-

sions and argue our points of view. I am about to get up and ask Sonya, Ruth and Sylvia what kind of shoes they would like, and whether they would get together with me to produce shoes, when Himbeck comes down our gangway. Just before my daydream I had noticed that a Greek woman and two Turkish women had upset some boxes and were sitting idle. Himbeck walks over to them and asks, 'Why aren't you working?' 'We're having a break,' they reply in unison. It is 1.45 p.m. and Himbeck is so caught off his guard by this response that he can only say, 'Well, so long as you make it a short one . . .' and disappears. The women mimic him as he goes and stay sitting down.

Thank God he's gone! Once a day Fatima and I visit one another. Today we use the supply of cardboard as our excuse, since I've got too much of it and she hasn't enough. 'Well,' she says, laying her hand on my shoulder, 'they're a lot of bandits here.' 'Bandits all right,' I say, 'though that's too nice a word for them.' We don't have time for more. Fatima claps me on the shoulder again and shoves the cardboard under her arm. I pull the drill over and watch her, in her red overalls, move slowly back to her work-bench.

I reach for the next lid, push it down over the jig, reach out again and insert the plastic window. I am still sitting here doing the same piecework.

Up near the ceiling long rows of recently sprayed and drying vacuum cleaners are moving along a belt among the neon lights. I feel wrung out, and only when I have whistled an old hit tune five or six times do I realize what it is. It's an old song which I haven't thought of for ten years. I didn't know that I still knew it: 'The pretty girls/with a faithful look/you'll find in every harbour. They'll give you/after every trip/a little bit of pleasure.' That's all I remember.

Jedina has got up with an armful of fitted lids which she puts in my box. We've never talked about it but she does it every day.

Have you ever seen a woman jump up and run to the lavatory

with a bag of cotton wool? No? Neither have I outside the factory. She soon comes back, stuffs the rest of the cotton wool into a box and goes on working at the carousel.

I must get up, so I go over to see Ruth. 'Look at that,' she says, and points to the tray in the carousel where the various screws are kept. The screws used to lie around in a lot of muck but they are now kept on some bright lilac foam stuff arranged by Kit, who thinks that looks nicer. She works with Ruth. 'Another half an hour,' I hear Ruth say as I go away.

When I sit down again I hear Alma telling another woman, who has been here as long as she has, that when the rate-fixer comes nobody will be able to run around any more. 'Everybody can walk around while they are working,' I yell, 'shopgirls . . .' 'Yes,' says the woman, 'but we're unskilled.' 'But we're not slaves,' I reply.

The noises slowly die down and there is gradually some movement in the building. Some women are recovering the use of their feet and are leaving their benches: the first pieceworkers have finished their piece-number for the day.

During the last twenty minutes each pieceworker has swept round her work-place and wiped her machine down with a wet cloth. They don't want dirty work-places. There are no paid women or men cleaners employed in factories, so the women pieceworkers have to do it themselves, for nothing.

Ruth comes to my bench with her green plastic bag and drops into my swivel chair. Her worst pains are in her feet, mine are in my left shoulder. Jedina has shoulder pains and daily headaches, when she gets home she lies down and takes two or three pain-killers. Sometimes she falls asleep and doesn't wake up till the morning, but usually she gets up after two or three hours. Sonya fetches her child from the kindergarten and then lies down for an hour. I get aggressive when the day's piecework is over, I am already spoiling for a fight by the lunch-break but I really let fly in the evening. I long for quiet, but I start quarrelling. The piece rhythm gets inside me and I can't switch it off like the machine. During the last few minutes I stand at my bench reading the morning's newspaper. You can't afford to clock off a minute early, otherwise it will be deducted from your pay. I go slowly down the stairs to the washroom where our things are hanging in the lockers. There I am assaulted by a mixture of smells and a babble of languages. I see women holding their feet under cold water, I see soapdishes of all colours, I see petticoats and breasts. Hangers fall to the floor because the women are getting dressed as quickly as they can. Everyone wants one thing only: to get away. Some of the foreign women are washing themselves quietly under warm water.

Reflection

I have described one working day, but I have done that once already when I wrote about my work as a fitter for AEG-Telefunken.

But why a whole day? Well, how can I describe daily piecework better without taking a great deal more space? For example, when I see one of the rare reports about industrial production on television or at the cinema, I never find out as much as I'd like to. You never get to see an entire work process, I've never seen a basic work-unit that hasn't been cut. I find myself still seeing the pieceworker long after other images have replaced her. Recently I saw a tantalizing movie made by a film-maker who spent the whole time moving around different factories. By the end of the film I had learned nothing from him. The second reason for presenting the whole day is in order to ask how women can resist the piece-numbers imposed upon them. I mean that it is necessary to present a whole day so that the terror visited on women by piecework can be understood.

The rate-fixer comes

Everything moves quite fast now, the rate-fixer is in the shop. Ruth, who is the first to see him, walks past Sonya, Sylvia and me and points him out to us.

The women have all consulted with one another and have decided to work slowly and to include all the secondary activities like fetching and replacing materials. We have our agreement, but the rate-fixer has his methods. This one, for example, simply turns his stopwatch off while the materials are being replenished, which is something that has to be done several times a day during piece-time.

I look where Ruth is pointing. There he is, a small man with a bald head and gold-rimmed spectacles. He stands, thumb on stopwatch, behind a living woman worker and times each of her hand movements with only one aim in view – to raise the piece-number.

A few days later this worker is one of the first to receive the new piece-number from the foreman. For the same wage she is now supposed to fit 400 pieces a day instead of 280. She gets her previous wage for one more week, but if after that she fails to produce the 400 and continues to produce 280, then she will earn DM 2 less an hour. The 280 pieces, for years the daily requirement, are suddenly called 'the old piece-number' by the rate-fixer, the foreman and the setter. The 'old piece-number' has done its job. For years it has been the product of a woman worker's labour, but it is now despised. It is not forbidden to talk about the 'old piece-number', but nobody does. The woman with the same number of parts to assemble with the same materials at the same machine has now to produce 120 extra pieces a day.

The individual pieceworkers are individually checked and their new piece-numbers are distributed individually. This makes it very difficult to fight collectively. There is individual resistance, but it remains just that because of the difficulty of comparing the rates, and it subsides very quickly. While new piece-numbers are being distributed daily, the first pieceworkers to be checked are already slaving away at their new numbers. Those who refuse are called to the office to see the foreman, who works out on a calculating machine how little they will be earning if they go on producing at the old rate. And the time for doing all this is chosen very carefully: just three weeks before the annual holiday. The firm banks on the women's desire to see their children and the issue is put very clearly – every woman knows what it is about. 'Do you want to get your holiday pay, see your child, come back to work here afterwards, or do you want to protest against the raising of the piece-numbers and get your notice while you are on holiday?'

Jedina will be seeing her children for the first time since Christmas. Kit has only her smallest child with her, her other three are in Turkey. A year ago another Turkish woman took her youngest child, born here, to her mother in Turkey because she had no one to look after it during the day, while she and her husband were working. So now all four of her children are living with their grandmother in Turkey. They did not go home for Christmas because they were saving up enough money to fly home in the summer and so have more time with their children. Over half the women in the factory are either from Yugoslavia or Turkey.

Then there is something else to keep the women quiet. Two days before the annual holiday you get your holiday pay. You will get in your hand 50 per cent of the previous month's earnings plus the 85 per cent paid in advance for the holiday month

117

of July 1975, which comes to more than you see at any other time. It is the money every woman in the shop has been counting on for weeks.

The next morning

The morning newspapers report sackings in the telephone section at Siemens and short time in the Berlin works of Osram. Renate, who works as a float, says as she reads the reports, 'Better less money here than no work at all.' Alma folds up the paper and says, 'Now things are getting serious.'

I have conjunctivitis from the talc. As soon as work begins everything shoots into action and the lids that I assemble disappear like hot cakes, it's just a race. The pieceworkers who take them from me have to pack them twenty to a box, but I can't keep up with them so they have to take batches of ten or five. This means that they have to run further to keep up their output and I lose the rhythm which every pieceworker builds up to get through her job. We are under stress from 6.30 a.m. and everyone in the building has been up since between 4 and 5 a.m.

After the first break the rate-fixer reaches Sonya, Sylvia and the whole group who work standing at individual machines. His arrival just after the first break is no accident, he knows that this is the time when the rate of production is at its highest. He tries to ingratiate himself just as he did everywhere else in the shop. Sonya and Sylvia refuse to join in his jokes and go on working quietly and slowly. Sylvia's riveter is going 'Bong bong bong bong', when her normal everyday rhythm is 'Bong-bong-bong-bong'. I don't need to look over, I can hear the tempo. All the same I do look, and Sylvia seems to be fighting with windmills, almost as if something were holding her back and preventing her from turning the containers round more quickly. She can't go on like that, I think to myself. I listen all the time and drill in the same rhythm as Sylvia's riveting. The rate-fixer puts up with this for twenty minutes, pulling a face the whole time. Just how does a rate-fixer deal with this kind of thing? The piece-number Sylvia is eventually given has nothing to do with the rate at which she was timed. He stood beside Sylvia like a trained dog with his thumb on the stopwatch, and almost had a heart attack when she took a handkerchief from her overall pocket and blew her nose.

The rate-fixer moves on to Sonya. Sylvia stands up coolly, laughs in my direction, lights a cigarette and smokes in peace.

The rate-fixer times the fastest worker at the carousel

Newspaper headline: 'Two thirds of unemployed women today are unskilled. In this situation women should use their rights under the labour claims law [*Arbeitsförderungsgesetz*].'

How? Even if a woman worker manages to get there, even if she has the energy and enough money, even if she is prepared to leave her piecework and get herself a skill, even if she can overcome the indifference and unfriendliness of the officials at the Labour Exchange, even if she manages to get and keep an appointment – even then, she still has to wait for six weeks to two months. How will she pass the test she is then put through? How will she answer the questions on a computer sheet within a fixed time limit? That is mockery and cynicism!

Here is a job advertisement from the *Berliner-Zeitung* of the same day as that headline.

Female packers wanted for deep freeze food.

Foreigners or women with small children need not apply.

Berolina-Tiefkühlkost, Reinickendorf, Winterstr. 24/25. Tel: 491 30 03.

Time control is used in the factory we work in. It is also used in DTW, Bosse, Telefunken, Krone, Gillette, Osram, Philips, and in countless smaller firms in the Berlin metal industry that are unknown to me.

The rate-fixer reaches Halime. She is Turkish, the fastest worker on the carousel, and the one who is most often ill. We are all watching her and we have all tried to impress on her that she must work slowly. The rate-fixer presses his stopwatch and Halime presses light bulbs into the vacuum cleaners. Monika, opposite Halime, starts up the same process in order to control Halime's speed. Now Halime is fixing switches to the motor cables – the rate-fixer stays glued to her heels.

I can't help thinking of the cotton-pickers' song from Traven's novel.[1] There they weigh the picker's load, here they time our every movement.

Song of the Cotton-Pickers

Cotton is worn by king and prince,
Millionaire and president,
But the lowly cotton-picker
Sweats to earn each bloody cent.
 Get going to the cotton field,
 The sun is moving up and up.
 Sling on your sack,
 Tighten your belt –
 Listen, the scales are turning.

Look at the food I get to eat –
Beans and chili, tortilla-bread –
And the scarecrow shirt I swiped,
Torn by bush and patched with shreds.

1. B. Traven, *Die Baumwollpflücker*, 1926; translated as *The Cotton-Pickers*, 1969; published in Great Britain by Allison & Busby, 1979

Get going to the cotton field,
The sun is moving on and on.
Sling on your sack,
Tighten your belt –
Listen, are the scales begging?

Cotton sells at soaring prices,
But I ain't got a decent shoe.
My pants hang down in ragged threads,
Here and there my butt shows through.
Get going to the cotton field,
The sun climbs high too soon.
Sling on your sack,
Tighten your belt –
Listen, are the scales bossing?

On my head a straw sombrero,
Kicked in when I got beat.
But I couldn't pick without it
Bending in the burning heat.
Get going to the cotton field,
The sun is aiming high.
Sling on your sack,
Tighten your belt –
Hey, are the scales trembling?

I'm just a lousy vagabond,
See, that's the way they made me be,
And there's no cotton crop for you
Unless it's picked by bums like me.
March! – in cotton-picking ranks
Beneath the firing sun!
Or fill your sacks with rocks –
Hear, are the scales breaking?

Halime needs some lids and comes over to me for them. 'You're too quick, dammit!' I say. 'Still too quick?' she asks. When I look up again I see Halime pushing completed vacuum cleaners onto the belt while Monika is only just beginning to assemble the lids. I hear Monika call out 'Halime'. She holds out a bag of sweets over the belt so as to be able tell Halime that she is working too fast again, and then at last I see her slowing down.

The following morning I learn that the rate-fixer will be coming either to Jedina or to me. We think that it will be Jedina because she is the faster worker. She has been on the same job for three years. She has a new machine which involves one additional hand movement, otherwise the only thing that has changed in that time is the colour of the individual parts. Any fair-minded person would assume that our piece-number would be reduced to allow for an additional movement every minute.

During the night I lay awake trying to think of ways of stopping the rate-fixer from coming into the shop at all. The noise around me is growing. The foreman is arguing with Sonya and Sylvia, I've never seen him talk so long to women workers before. Afterwards I go over to them and ask what's up. Sonya screams – they've been given their new piece-number. Starting at once, they have to produce 1,400 containers a day. So far they have been producing 800 a day, which together with the 150 produced by the afternoon shift made 950 altogether.

Sonya told the foreman that if the firm stuck to the new piece-number she'd go. To which he replied that at DM 7 an hour he could get all the women he needed, people were being sacked everywhere. Sonya has been in this factory for two and a half years. She is riveting while she is telling me all this. I am standing by her bench when the rate-fixer addresses me: 'No doubt your piece-number is too good as well. I shall time you.' I ask, 'What are you really after?' The rate-fixer replies, 'I am registering the fact that you are just standing about talking.'

Subsequently he turns up, and while his watch is going I get up and stack materials, first the metal plates, then the glass windows. I haven't even got any rubber stoppers when he interrupts me, saying, 'Start using your materials.' I start working and say nothing. I assemble slowly, but what real difference does that make to a woman's piecework? If I work in slow motion then I can turn a rate of one piece per minute into a rate of one every one minute twenty seconds. Now I am sweating with the effort to assemble everything slowly, whereas normally we knock everything together and chase our piece-number for eight hours flat. I pick up a metal plate knowing very well that normally I would pick them up five at a time. I prolong each movement, I tell myself to work slowly. Am I working slowly enough? Is there any chance at all with the rate-fixer standing over me?

After twenty pieces the rate-fixer moves from me to Jedina, and she sets to. I start at the same time, but she leaves me behind. While I am still drilling, Jedina is reaching for the metal plate. I hear all this, I haven't yet turned round. Jedina's drill is screeching, and if the screw doesn't fit properly then she knocks it in with the drill. What has gone wrong? We have discussed the rate-fixing so many times. The rate-fixers are positioned differently with Jedina. The senior man has a trainee with him, and he isn't standing with the old man as he did when they were with me, but next to Jedina so that she has one on each side of her. She feels surrounded. I turn round and see that she is trembling. The rate-fixer measures twenty pieces with Jedina, as he did with me. She keeps up her speed.

'What went wrong, why were you so quick, Jedina?' 'Marianne, I was afraid.' 'What of?' I ask her. 'I don't know, but I was afraid the whole time.' She then tells me that although she has worked in several different factories in Germany for seven years this is the first time that she has come across a rate-fixer. She is surrounded by other women workers, they're all shouting at her for working so quickly. She bursts out suddenly: 'If you

123

don't stop it, if you don't stop it, I'll ask the rate-fixer to come back and then I'll really work fast. I wasn't working fast today. I've been at this place for three years, I can't go slowly.'

Rationalized out

Three days later Jedina and I are called to see the foreman. Starting from now we are told to assemble 651 pieces a day, 171 more than before.

When we were producing 480 pieces a day we were earning DM 8.10 an hour. From now on we will only get DM 5.90 an hour for 480 pieces. For 500 pieces we will get DM 6.14, for 520 we will get DM 6.39 and for 651 pieces a day DM 8. They might just as well have given us a target of 1,200 instead of 651, it would be no more remote. The older pieceworkers shake their heads, they say that there's no point in arguing.

Ruth is not at her bench and I ask Jedina and Sonya if they'd like to come with me. They don't come because they too say that it won't change anything. I leave the shop to go and see the Works Council representative. There's a card pinned up on his office door saying that he is available to see people twice a week for half an hour. Someone who knows where he is gets him to the telephone and I make an appointment to see him. An hour later I am once again at the door, but it is closed. I sit down on a pallet outside and decide to stay there until he arrives. The area the offices lead off from is enormous. I can see where two skilled workers are assembling deep freezes. One of them eats a mouthful out of his lunch-box every time he passes it while working. For the first time in a long while I see human beings again, people working in the technical offices who stop and talk when they meet one another – they have the time to talk.

Half an hour later the door opens. A Works Council meeting has been taking place while I've been thinking there's no one in there. They had locked themselves in. I put the piece-number increase to the Works Council Chairman and demand a re-assessment in the presence of the Piece Commission of the Works Council. I don't like asking for more time measurement because I don't like timing at all, but I do want to lodge a protest. I want to do something about an increase which means a time of under a minute a piece. The Chairman of the Works Council says that I would be doing my workmates no good by applying to the Piece Commission, I should leave it alone and look around me, nowhere else are women paid DM 8. His behaviour is the same as at the last factory meeting. Everything he had to say was the same as his speech about the May rate of DM 8. When he finished that speech he quickly declared the meeting closed so that no woman got the chance to speak. If you ever see him on the shopfloor he will be distributing a little sheet as fast as he can go. It is *Impulse*, the newspaper about safety at work. Shoulders hunched, he creeps among the rows of women handing out the paper. His name is Gundlach. When I am back at my bench, Himbeck turns up. He is on his way to becoming the new worker director and has been creeping around the shop for months. With notebook and pencil he has been spying on every worker. I've seen him checking on the rate-fixer with a stopwatch, and even sticking his nose into dustbins to make sure that we're not hiding scrap.

Himbeck is terrified by my visit to the Works Council: nothing can be taken for granted in a women's factory. 'With the new piece-number you'll never make the money you were earning before,' he says, pausing beside me. 'So you know as well as I do,' I say, 'that the new rate is unmanageable.' Himbeck: 'It is no longer humanly possible. Perhaps you can do it for a short while, but you won't keep it up. The women's wages were too high here.' Herr Himbeck is not as much of a coward as the Works Council Chairman Gundlach. I tell Jedina what Himbeck has said. She replies, 'Marianne, you'll see, after our holiday everything will be as it was before.' Two days later, thirty women get their notice; Ruth and I are among them. The rate-fixer has left the shop, the piece-numbers are raised throughout, and as a result fewer workers are needed. Notices are handed out: 'We hereby terminate the labour contract concluded with you on account of a reduction in production.' I had just got mine. Somebody from the personnel office, in cream-coloured gaberdine trousers, had been standing among us as we worked. Since he wasn't normally there I knew what it was all about. The foreman had to hand out the notices, fifteen minutes before the weekend and eight days before the holiday promised to us. I say, 'Jedina, I've got my notice.' 'It's not true,' she says. 'Come here and read it for yourself,' I say. I call out the news to Sonya and Sylvia, older workers hear it and come over. Fatima, separated from me by the entire shop, has heard about it and arrives. The women are shocked. They stand around my bench in a thick cluster but disperse as soon as we hear the first women clocking off.

A few weeks later – after the holiday – there are more notices, more women are thrown out onto the street. Sonya and Sylvia are among them; they have worked in this factory for two and a half and one and a half years respectively. They couldn't sack Fatima because she was having her fourth child.

First the rate-fixer, then an increase in piece-numbers or a speed-up on the line, fewer workers having to produce more, and finally mass sackings – this is what happens to women workers, this is what is happening now as I write this account, and it has been going on since the beginning of the present economic crisis. In the Berlin metal industry, I know it's happening at Siemens, AEG-Telefunken, Krone, Gillette, Philips, Osram and DTW.

From the city I live in come constant reports of the sacking of women workers – but there are also reports of demands, of resistance, of strikes by women!

I'm a ring-spinner – we've been rationalized too (1931)

I'm single and I live with my married sister and I look after the entire household. We are three adults and two children. As my brother-in-law does not earn enough to cover the living expenses of the family, my sister has to work, even though she is not well. To make things easier for her I see to the housekeeping as well as my job. I always get up at 5.45 a.m. Work begins at 6.30 a.m. I live opposite the spinning mill so I only need five minutes to get there. But before my morning's work at the factory begins, I get through some of the housework first. Once the factory gates have closed behind me, I am just a factory worker. If you are on the Works Council and the Health Insurance Board, working in the factory causes you a lot more work and anger. One workmate or another comes with complaints about wages or about being transferred to a different job. Then there are disputes with the foreman and the senior foreman. I'm a ring-spinner: we've been rationalized too. You can't talk about reasonable work here any more. Everything moves at high speed, it's all a miserable slog. Originally there were 28 ring-spinners in the shop, now we are 15 plus a relief column of seven girls. If one of us is away, the others have to do her work. With this speed-up they get increased output from us which is not reflected in our wages. This hardly stimulates pleasure or interest in our work. The machine and its owner are merciless, forcing us again and again into drudgery.

I have a quarter-of-an-hour breakfast-break. There's not much time for eating, you have to swallow rather than chew.

I get no rest during the one-hour lunch-break, instead I start preparing the evening meal. Then the little girl comes home from school and needs to change her clothes. In the afternoon she is left to her own devices. It hurts her to have her clothes changed because she is partly paralysed on the right side. The boy comes home in the evening, he stays at school. At 1 p.m., unrested, I am back at the machine until work finishes at 4.45 p.m. Then the household gets its turn. We sit and talk and the work has to wait. Each working day ends at 11 or 11.30 p.m.

E.L., aged 28[1]

1. From *Mein Arbeitstag – Mein Wochenende. 150 Berichten von Textilarbeiterinnen* [*My Working Day – My Weekend: 150 Reports from Women Textile Workers*]. collected and published by the German Textile Workers' Union, Berlin, 1931

My name is Pfeil-Rosar

*1975 was declared Women's Year. On 10 December 1975 there was
a ninety-minute television broadcast entitled: 'Is the End of Men's
Rule in Sight?' One woman tells them what is really wrong:*

My name is Pfeil-Rosar, I am 53 and a Works Councillor. I've
also been in the Union for twenty years, Herr Vetter! It hasn't
given me a penny, though. On the payroll I am described as a
shorthand typist, while the man next to me is a supervisor. But
one really shouldn't pretend that it's not an accident of birth.
Just look at what's been expected of me during my life! When
I was young I was told that I should have as many children as
possible, blond and blue-eyed. I didn't quite manage that
because they grew up dark. Then when the war came I was soon
called up and made to do men's work. And after the war – forgive
me for mentioning it – we women were only good enough for
cleaning up, clearing away the rubble. And then I had to disappear into the home. When I began looking for work in the '50s
I was chased out everywhere. I was told, 'We don't take
married women.' And we seem to have reached the same point
again. Today I am faced with the problem of being a woman
Works Councillor who has to sack women, because this so-called
recession affects women's jobs first of all. I have to beg my male
colleagues to consider other possibilities. They are pleasant
enough men in themselves, but as soon as women are mentioned
they turn into patriarchs from the last century, I promise you.
And what arguments can I use if even the women themselves say,
'Well, send us home then, we earn less than the men.' We can't

even turn that the other way round, so please tell me – what am I supposed to do today?

Merseburger: Are you talking about the special problem of female unemployment?

Pfeil-Rosar: What I'm talking about is the way we are always fetched out or sent home just as it suits the economy, and that we are just not prepared to let this happen to us any more. We are people too, and we have a right to work too, and we shouldn't any longer have to depend on men to look after us.

Merseburger: Isn't this question addressed not just to Herr Vetter but to . . . ?

Pfeil-Rosar: The question is addressed in the first place to Herr Vetter, because as a Union member I have found every door closed and no one to help me. Neither my Works Council colleagues nor the Union, and yet we have Section 75 of the Factory Act. But it's not worth the paper it's printed on.

Vetter: I can only partly agree with my colleague, if she is having a difficult time during the present economic recession.

Working conditions: living conditions

1. Being an unskilled woman worker means lifelong discrimination which extends to every area of life. For me, to be given unskilled piecework every day is like giving a woman who can read and write only eight letters of the alphabet to use. It means forcing a woman who could be a turner, a toolmaker or a carpenter to assemble five to twenty components a minute, to punch, to fold, to weld.

Women's thinking and expressive powers get stunted by piecework, by producing anything from 400 to 5,000 items daily – for years, for decades. 'Unskilled women workers': this is the last time I shall use that designation, since it too is discriminatory, because it is clear that it is the capitalist system which is responsible for the fact that in the Federal Republic 3·3 million out of 3·5 million women workers have no skills.

Women in the factories of the Federal Republic cannot acquire skills, nor can we have any sense of achievement in our work.

Women's inventiveness, our curiosity and strength, our aptitudes, our anger, our longings, our love and our courage are all drained away by piecework.

2. In the factories of the Federal Republic our starting wage is still less than DM 6 an hour. Hourly wages of DM 6 or DM 7 are only obtainable by piecework, which has to be kept up every day. The wages of women workers are 30 per cent lower than those of their male counterparts. According to one statistical survey (the micro-census of March 1971), 71·1 per cent of women workers received a net income of DM 600 a month, 28·7 per cent one of DM 600 to 1,200, and 0·2 per cent one of DM 1,200 or more.

A woman's earnings are still seen as supplementary and are not enough to enable her to live independently. This puts women workers among the most dependent and the most exploited. The economic necessity which drives them to do this work, which stops them from leaving until their daily piece-number is reached, and the responsibility and dependence involved in having children, tie them to the factory.

3. Women workers are the first to be sacked. This has always been so and is again in the present crisis. It happened before in the 1966–7 recession. During the two World Wars women were conscripted and worked for fourteen hours a day, including Sundays, in the mines, in every kind of heavy labour and in skilled work, at the same time as being underfed. Then when the wars were over they were sent back into the home again.

I haven't been able to get the figures for women who have been sacked or who are unemployed during the present crisis. Labour Exchanges and the trade unions keep what they know about these things to themselves.

Many women, and it is not known just how many, who are married and whose husbands are earning do not register as unemployed.

If a woman worker registers as unemployed, her unemployment benefit is calculated on the basis of her last wage. The wage of a working woman is from 30 to 35 per cent lower than that of a working man. I know a 46-year-old woman worker who was getting, in December 1975, an unemployment benefit of DM 511.20 a month after working in factories for fifteen years. Her gross earnings in her last factory were DM 900.

Unemployment relief, which is what is available when unemployment benefit can no longer be claimed, is paid to unemployed married women only when there is 'need'. Whether or not the sacked and now unemployed woman gets any money has nothing to do with her years of work and output, but only to do with the wage her husband earns. An unemployed woman cannot stipulate where she will work or what that work will be, she cannot even look around like better-paid people. She must take the next job that is offered to her as quickly as possible, just in order to live. And she has to take the next job even if the work is worse than what she was doing before or even if she has to work further away from where she lives or no matter what other disadvantages there are.

4. A woman worker is not paid more for her years of experience as she gets older. In fact she is usually so worn out by piecework that she is paid less as she gets older simply because she can no longer keep up the pace. It is also a fact that women over the age of 35 are rarely able to change factories, because the personnel departments of the large factories won't take on women of this age.

5. Pregnant women are not taken on. Women are asked if they are pregnant when they apply for a job, and their answer is frequently checked by a urine test. If a woman is already employed and then gets pregnant, she must be given, by law, a job outside the piece system. But she will earn the same money only if she has spent a long time in the factory and has a good piece average. Despite the law, some women go on with piecework when they are pregnant just to improve their average. I have seen women doing this well into their fourth or fifth month because they need the money. I have heard foremen lying to women who insisted on their right to a non-piecework job, saying that there were none available.

6. Another result of the super-exploitation that piecework is, another result of the total mental and physical exhaustion it produces, is that when the weekend comes at last women cannot make use of the medical services available to them. For example, in the evening, after a day's piecework, I was in no state to go

and have my teeth filled or have an inflamed tendon dealt with. Neither were the women next to me. The necessary equipment is there and the factory pays if you make a claim, but after eight hours' piecework the workers, both women and men, often do not have the energy to go to the doctor.

In times of economic crisis women and men will go on working even if they feel unable to do so. They will even postpone operations for fear of being sacked.

7. Women pieceworkers are always given the worst tools and the worst machines to work with. The materials they are expected to use get worse all the time because of management's perpetual effort to get things made more cheaply. Is there a factory anywhere in which the workers, male or female, have ever successfully demanded that the materials they work on should be improved?

8. From the age of sixty women workers get a pension which is too small to live on. The pension is so low because it is based on women's working wages. For their entire lives women will have been among the lowest paid of workers, so that: 'The average pension ceiling for women who paid contributions into the Workers' Pension Insurance Fund for 40 to 45 years came to DM 356.70; those women who were insured for 40 to 50 years could, on the other hand, expect an average pension of DM 436.40.'[1]

1. Renate Meyer-Harter, *Die Stellung der Frau in der Sozialversicherung* [*The Position of Women in Social Insurance*], Berlin, 1974

The cost of potatoes

I go out shopping and see how the price of potatoes has changed overnight:

At Mann's[1] 2·5 kilos of Ackergold potatoes cost DM 3.98
          2·5 kilos of Bintje potatoes cost DM 3.68
At Kaiser[1] 2·5 kilos of German Class 1 potatoes cost DM 2.98
          2·5 kilos of Bintje potatoes cost DM 3.78

I am not paying three or four marks for two and a half kilos of potatoes, so I go to the shops where they are sold loose and that amount costs only DM 2.70. They only have this one variety of German potato. At the end of October I bought a 50-kilo sack from a woman in one shop and paid DM 17 for them. I ask her how much 50 kilos cost now and the answer is DM 54. I ask what potatoes cost after 1945. 'Young woman,' she says, 'I'll look that up for you at home in my old accounts.' I ask for five kilos, and the woman takes first one and then another forkful and shakes them into the scales. As I hold out my plastic bag I think to myself that I can even count them as they go in, and I've got to pay DM 4.50 for them.

A week later I ask her if she has looked up her old accounts. She says that 50 kilos of potatoes cost DM 60 immediately after the war. The 50-kilo sacks which cost DM 54 a week ago cost DM 58 today.

3 February 1976

1. Both Mann and Kaiser are Berlin supermarkets.

Women workers strike at Pierburg

In November 1975 I saw the film *Your Struggle is Our Struggle*, which was shown at the Technological University of Berlin. It is a film about women workers on strike at Pierburg, which produces almost all the carburettors and fuel pumps for the West German car industry. Of the 3,800 people employed there, 70 per cent are foreign workers and more than 2,500 of the total are women. A poster advertising the film has an extract from the script printed on the back:

In 1970 the women workers in Wage-group 1 went on strike to get it done away with. Two days before Whitsun 1973, the rest of the women went on strike with the following demands:

1. Wage-group 2 must disappear and all women in it are to be up-graded to Group 3.

2. Those who have been employed in the factory longer must be paid more than new workers.

3. As there are no clean working areas in the factory, everyone must be paid a supplement for dirty work.

4. All workers, women and men, to get a rise of DM 1 an hour.

5. Women who work on special machines to be re-graded to Wage-group 5.

6. The time lost on this meeting to be paid for.

7. All women doing heavy physical work in this factory must be paid at the same rate as men.

8. Dismissals for frequent illness must cease.

9. Overtime to be distributed fairly.

10. If someone falls ill and has to go to the doctor, then she or he should get half a day a month off without loss of pay for this purpose.

11. One paid day a month to be housewives' day.

12. Travel expenses must be improved significantly.

13. We demand the immediate dismissal of Foreman Gromes and Personnel Director Biecker.

After two days, when management had agreed to negotiations, work was resumed. The Works Council proposed that 2,400 workers should be re-graded, but nothing happened.

In the summer of 1973 a widespread and spontaneous strike movement broke out in West Germany for cost-of-living increases. In August the Pierburg women came out again demanding the abolition of Wage-group 2 and a rise of DM1 an hour. After a strike of five days, Wage-group 2 was abolished and the women who had been in it were given 65 pfennigs an hour more. Male and female workers in Wage-groups 3 to 10 got 53 pfennigs an hour more. Thirty-one dismissed women had to be taken back and four out of the five strike days were paid for.

As I watch the striking women in the film – their bodies swaying to the slogans they are shouting – I feel that their struggle goes beyond their immediate demands.

I was delighted by the women and looked forward to the discussion after the film. I wanted to ask them if their working conditions had improved as a result of the strike, what those conditions were like, whether they had a rate-fixer in their factory and if so what they had done about him. None of the workers took part in the discussion, only four Works Councillors. I still want to ask those questions!

Women in struggle at Lip

In that same year, 1973, the two-year struggle of women and men in the French factory of Lip began. What the women have to say about that struggle can be read in their pamphlet.[1] Among their points are these:

On learning to speak: 'I arranged things with my workmates, but only with women. In my opinion it was better so because we could talk more directly and concretely to one another . . . because we didn't use any big political words.'

About the factory: 'Back to the factory – that's what we all wanted . . . We loved the factory.'

About culture: 'We discovered that the people have their own culture filled with realism and humour. I'm thinking of the performance of Dario Fo and his troupe. It made such a pleasant change when this artist told us about the Italian style of struggle at our plenary meeting.' And: 'What have I, as a woman, learnt during this conflict? The first thing is the value of living collectively.'

What are the women's working conditions like? Are they any better after the fight? Is the piece-number any lower, or the speed of the assembly line any slower? Do the women have any more breaks? Can those who are semi-skilled become skilled? If so, what kind of training do they receive? What arrangements are there for children while their mothers are being trained?

I read in the pamphlet:

77 per cent of the semi-skilled workers at Lip are women who have

1. Published in German as *Wir Frauen von Lip – Frauen im Kampf* [*We Women of Lip – Women in Struggle*], Dietzenbach, 1975

almost no hope of promotion ... There are women who have been working at Lip for twenty years and are still semi-skilled.

And the worst thing about it all is that women's wages are looked on as 'supplementary', so that not only do women have harder working conditions – they work on the line – but they are also lower paid. A large number of working-class men accept this discrimination ... The real problem is that of qualifications: women are in the lowest wage-group because they are inadequately trained and are denied any chance of self-improvement. So this is the territory they must fight over ... We must realize that what matters most is to fight together for better working conditions, for better wages and for the recognition that we are not just 'women working for pin-money'.

Here are reports from two women who, after the struggle of Lip, are still doing the same jobs:

I make 800 pieces an hour

I made tiny parts in the clock department on very hard piece-work. It took me a year to get used to it. I had just lost my husband and was left with four children, so I couldn't do anything else. The work was both uninteresting and exhausting. I made tiny parts for the batteries of electric clocks. I know that because I made a point of finding out. I'd never have known otherwise, and I don't want to die a complete idiot. I cut platinum strips into small one-millimetre pieces – seven to eight thousand an hour. I would work on this for one to two hours because the quicker it went the less awful it felt. Then I would place each individual part on the plate, rub it smooth, pick it up with a kind of needle-point and put it into a shaping machine. If they were not clean enough I'd have to take them out again, rub them a little more and repeat the process.

Then I'd be finished. On average I had to complete 800 pieces an hour. It was awful how quickly you had to move your fingers ...

From Hand to Mouth

I'm horrified at the idea of having to go on with this work and
I've noticed that recently my eyes have got worse; when I go
back I shall apply for some other job. But I won't do that until
everybody is back, because I don't want to take anyone's job.
I'll have to hold on, but I shall ask then because I don't think I
can go on doing this painful, boring and inhuman work which
won't let you do anything with your hands except what the
machine demands.

Alice

I sit in front of my microscope with a pile of little parts

I had mixed feelings when I learned that I would be reinstated.
First I had a certain fear. It meant for me the end of the freedom
which had helped us to develop: a fraternal freedom, a freedom
of expression, a form of culture which we acquired talking to
all those who visited Lip. Now conformity and punctuality
would return – getting up early, running to work, rushing home
in the evening to start a new day with your husband and children. In other words, I would once again become dependent on a
society which doesn't give us the time to think.

That was a step backwards . . . But there was another feeling.
There was pride in having won a hard battle. Every returning
Lip worker would be another small victory anticipating the big
victory for which we have fought, and for which we shall fight
to the finish. Then I went into the factory. Only a few of us are
there, scattered about. I sit in front of my microscope with a pile
of little parts which I have to check . . . day after day.

Once again I am the little thing in front of its machine. But the
great friendship which arose during the struggle is still alive,
and in the ten-minute break we run joyfully to one another to
tell the latest news . . . and what our fellow-workers outside are
saying. Above all, to talk about what we are all feeling. We no

longer worry about whether someone is working in production or
in an office. I find this achievement very important. We must
preserve it, for it will be our strength.

Reine J.
September 1974

Fatima after the factory

I visited her in her flat in Schöneberg[1] in November. The street-lights are already lit and I stand in the street because no one is in. I wait – she can't fail to come, she has three children to look after. When she arrives it is her walk I recognize first: I have watched her walk away in the factory so often. She kisses me by way of greeting and I ask her, 'Are you having a child?' 'Yes Maria, it is heavy.'

Fatima was overweight even before her pregnancy. She has water in the legs and climbing the stairs up to her flat on the fourth floor makes her breathe heavily. She doesn't move at all in a portly way even though she is so heavy. I always admired that in the factory.

It is cold in the flat. She has two rooms and a kitchen for the five of them and the rent is DM 120. Her husband has built a bath in a recess in the kitchen. While I used to go home dirty at the end of a day in the factory, Fatima would spend a long time in the changing room washing herself thoroughly in warm water.

She gets up at 5 a.m. each day, and it is now 5 p.m. She lights the fire and I carry her shopping into the kitchen. As we move about we pick up bits of children's clothing scattered on the floor. Then we settle into armchairs. Fatima puts her feet up and we eat mandarins which I've got in my pocket. I ask about work. Fatima isn't on piecework any more, she is sticking numbers on vacuum cleaners now. I ask what the others are doing, but she doesn't understand me too well. Basically we get on by her telling me things, and when I don't understand what she says I ask again and she tells me once more. It emerges that for

1. A district of Berlin

the first three or four months of her pregnancy she stayed on piecework. I'm not sure whether she left it until then to say that she was pregnant or whether she did so straight away and was only given another job later. What does become clear is that she is earning the same wage as she was getting during her last month's piecework. Fatima has been in the factory for two years and has a good average. I ask which of the other women are still there and Fatima tells me which of them have been sacked. She talks at length about Mustafa's wife and is angry when I can't remember her. She too has been sacked.

Then Fatima says that there are now men working on the carousels. This news brings me to my feet. The men came from the deep-freeze department which had been closed down. They would never manage the piece system and would give notice, but then new men would be taken on and trained for it. Having only seen women working at the carousel, rushing about and out of breath, I feel like going to see with my own eyes men assembling parts at it. For a moment this idea has a liberating effect. I wonder how it affects the women sitting in the shop. I only saw women rushed off their feet, but now they'll be seeing men who can't manage the piecework.

We want coffee, but all the crockery has been used so we go to wash up. The kitchen is an icy hole. 'Cold, my sweet,' says Fatima, and points to two holes in the window pane. These have been made by children opposite shooting at it with a catapult. A piece of plastic covering the holes is blowing about in the draught. Fatima lends me a knitted jacket. We pile up the crockery and throw away the left-overs. Fatima curses her two older sons for not helping. 'Yesterday I cleaned everything, Maria. Every day cleaning, Maria. Husband working. I working, cleaning, cooking, washing children, also cleaning shirts, oh Maria!' Wiping the table Fatima finds two cellulose rags stained with blood. To me they look like the swabs left by a doctor after taking a blood test. I tell her this, but Fatima points to a roll of cellulose hanging on the kitchen wall. She's right, it's the same. She tries to work out what has happened to her children. The last she saw of the big ones was at five o'clock this morning. She goes to the dustbin and turns it out. No blood-stains there, so she sweeps it all up again. The water for the washing-up gradually gets hotter. Fatima unpacks her bag and takes out a new glass coffee pot – two similar ones have already been broken – and a thick, heavy bundle of parsley. She shows me how to pack it into the fridge properly so that it will stay fresh for a week. She says that now that she is pregnant her husband does the shopping every day, so she no longer has to carry heavy loads.

Fatima's husband, Cemal, arrives just as we are finishing the washing-up. He greets me as if he knew me and unpacks the several plastic bags he is carrying. Fatima starts to cook a soup of tomatoes, noodles, a Turkish spice I don't know, and beef stock.

Murat, aged six and the youngest son, comes home from kindergarten with a lantern he has made himself. He lights his lantern and switches off the living-room light. Above the sofa there is a large map of Turkey in bright colours. Murat kneels on the sofa holding the lantern high above his head and shows me his home town, deep in the south of Turkey. In between times I go and help Fatima with the cooking. Cemal goes out again to buy a needle for the record player and some Turkish salami. Murat is hungry and opens a tin of sardines and shares them with me before the meal.

The two older ones are not yet home, but since Cemal doesn't eat on his building site, nor Fatima at the factory, they don't wait to start the meal. On the table are slices of white bread, baked by Fatima, a plate of salami and ham, yesterday's warmed-up spaghetti, and in the middle the pot of soup, in which the dominant colours are red and green. Beside each plate is a bunch of parsley and I watch Fatima to see how you eat it. She draws the whole stem through her mouth, chewing off the leaves till nothing but the bare stem is left.

We don't talk much during the meal because everyone is hungry. Every so often Cemal turns over the small Turkish records, and Murat tells his mother about the kindergarten. He speaks fluent German with a Berlin accent. Whenever he senses that his mother doesn't understand him he switches to Turkish. Next year he goes to school. He was born in Berlin, in a hospital in Schöneberg, and Fatima would like to go there again for her confinement. The hospital was good, but the births have always been difficult and she is afraid of this happening again. In fact that was the first thing we talked about when we were sitting in the armchairs. She didn't want this child but she couldn't tolerate the pill. After the birth of the fourth child she wants a coil fitted to protect her from the 'baby doctor'.

Fatima has put her feet up again, her eyes look small. Since I am trying to describe her, I think I shall ask her if I can take her photograph. It is Thursday and Fatima has two more days' work – at the moment Saturdays are being worked in preparation for Christmas. Her maternity leave begins in January.

I feel really warm after the hot soup. Murat has brought out toys from under the sofa – aeroplanes and ships. I'd like to stay sitting in the armchair because it feels good. I only go because I know they both have to leave at 5 a.m. Cemal, who works on a building site, has turned on the news to hear the weather report. The first snowfall is forecast for tomorrow.

Women on piecework

'What is skilled work? Work which carries within itself the seed of further development. Work which is able to set in motion the intellectual and – at best – the creative powers of the working person.

'And what is unskilled work? Dead work: work which when ended is also finished with, work which does not relate in any stimulating way to the being of the worker . . .

'In earlier times there was no unskilled work in the strict sense; it was first made necessary by the development of industry, with its division and mechanization of the work process, its enormous expansion of engineering, its need for a cheap labour force which, so it seemed at first, could be left totally untrained with impunity.'[1]

'There are three of us working at a fish-saw. For eight hours a day I have to lift 24-pound slabs of fish from the pallet to the table and take them out of their paper wrappings. You bend down, heave up the heavy slab, drop it with a bang on the table, pull off the paper, turn round, bend down again, heave up the next one, let it bang down on the table, take off the paper, turn around, pull up another, and so it goes on, hour after hour, the 24-pound slab.'[2]

'At F's I had to collect, pack and despatch punch cards, which I took from the machines. Mostly I just had to collect them. A

1. Dr Marie Baum, *Die Folgen ungelernter Arbeit für die Arbeiterin* [*The Consequence of Unskilled Labour for the Working Woman*], 1910
2. Regina Korn, 'Weihnachtszeit bei Findus', in *Liebe Kollegin* ['Christmas at Findus', in *Dear Colleague*], 1973

terribly boring and enervating job, not much better than at
W & B's. On the machine at F's it went like this: collect, collect,
collect, wait, stare, wait, collect, collect, collect – and again,
collect, wait, stare, collect, wait, stare, collect.'[3]

'In the left hand a tacho casing, in the right two bolts. Bolts
into the casing, casing over a massive block, block over the rivet-
pins, rivet-pins onto the bolt-heads by pressing a lever with the
right foot. With the right hand put the riveted tacho casing into
a box, with the left . . .'[4]

'In the grinding shop I worked at three machines simul-
taneously. I was rushing all the time to get through the piece-
number. The whole time I was standing with one foot on the
pedal. We always had our hands in petroleum jelly to prevent
scratches when the diamond passed through. The steam made
your hair greasy. I couldn't help coughing. It was 39 degrees C.
in summer. I was so afraid of not keeping up that I produced
more than was necessary, 1,500 to 1,800 pieces a day. I didn't
write down the excess pieces in case they made us do even more.'[5]

'Frau Heinrich's work goes in short cycles. You can tell that
by the boxes stacked up in front of her which make up her day's
task. She almost disappears behind them. Her work-cycle lasts
for nine seconds. She takes a base, picks up a support with a
pair of tweezers and welds the support to the base. She does the
same with the second support and puts the finished base in the
box. To be able to go on with this Frau Heinrich has extended

3. 'Eine Frau in der Revolte' ['A Woman in Revolt'], in Heiner Dorroch,
Wer die Gewalt sät [*Whoever Sows Violence*], 1974

4. Alice Schwarzer, 'VDO-Akkordarbeiterin Nr. 3444', in *Frauenarbeit –
Frauenbefreiung* ['VDO Pieceworker No. 3444', in *Women's Work – Women's
Liberation*], 1973

5. Jeanne D., aged 51, semi-skilled worker, in *Gegen die linken Phallo-
kraten. Frauen bei Lip* [*Against the Left Phallocrats: Women at Lip*], Merve
Verlag, 1975

her movements over the years, within the limits of piecework. She has invented a few additional movements, but still manages to get through the required amount of work. She doesn't simply pick up the materials and weld them together beneath the electrode. If you watch her you see that she spreads out her arms as if she were flying, draws them together and picks up the materials with both hands as if she had come upon them by pure chance. As she does this she rocks backwards and forwards, treads on the foot pedal three or four times, and only then welds the first part. Then out go the arms again. Frau Heinrich uses all this to help her get through her piecework, otherwise it would be superfluous movement and she couldn't afford it. She does exactly the same thing with her feet. She has to weld two spots on every unit, while the other women have to do from ten to twelve. But here again Frau Heinrich adds a few movements. While she picks up the pieces and before she puts them under the electrode she rocks up and down three or four times on the foot pedal, and only then does the real welding.

Frau Heinrich has developed these movements in resistance to the inhuman piecework. A unit is processed every nine seconds. Frau Heinrich welds 3,140 tube bases a day.'[6]

6. Marianne Herzog: see the chapter, 'Welding tubes: an eight-hour day', in this book

Postscript

I am thirty-nine years old and it took me thirty years to wake up. I was born in Mecklenburg in the DDR and grew up in a small town where for eight years I went to school. At the age of fifteen I began a three-year apprenticeship in a state-owned bookshop. The day after my apprenticeship finished I left the DDR and went to the West. The small town in which I grew up had become too small and the books available in the bookshop were not enough. I wanted to read more, to see more. That was in 1957 and the Wall did not yet exist.

I travelled to East Berlin and from there took the local train to West Berlin and then went on by another train to a West German provincial town. I had applied for a job in a bookshop there while I was still in the DDR, and they had accepted me. I worked there for about two years, read a lot, made up for lost time, hitch-hiked through the Federal Republic (I knew nothing of West Germany apart from the town in which I worked), took casual jobs and worked in vineyards during the harvest as I travelled, thumbed my way to Paris and lived and worked in a household there for three months. After this I decided to go back to the DDR because I loved the people there and had missed them, especially those of my own age, the whole time I was in the West. I returned to the DDR and told them my story. I had to hand in my passport and, together with others who wanted to return to the DDR, was put in a transit camp in Mecklenburg.

I was held in the camp for several weeks. I thought that the interrogations (the first I had ever undergone), the camp life, the refusal to let me go to the town I was heading for, were all due to a mistake or a misunderstanding by the administrators of the camp. However, I still wanted to go back. I volunteered to work in the fields and waited for the results of the checking procedures. We were all asked the same questions: Are there any legal proceedings against you in the West? Are you accused of something? Are you in debt? Are you involved in a divorce? After about a month to six weeks I was released from the camp and sent to a town I had never been to before, a town in which I had no friends. I married a childhood friend, not because I wanted to, but more because I had to find somewhere to live. We lived in one room, sleeping on a camp bed and an air mattress – nothing else would fit into it. We had no kitchen and no toilet. We soon quarrelled. I was unable to find any work in my profession. Instead of working in a bookshop I worked for an insurance company as a claims clerk, transforming accidents that human beings had suffered into insurance claims. I worked out how much money a person who had been involved in an accident would get for a damaged or lost organ – mutilations into sums of money. A two-roomed flat was allocated to us, together with another young married couple – we did not know each other. We now had a larger room and shared a kitchen. Just at the moment when the firm had delegated me to go to a school (I had always wanted to go back to school), I became pregnant. Abortions were illegal in the DDR until 1972.

It was only in West Berlin that I could find a doctor willing to perform an abortion. As I walked down the stairs after he had examined me, a note with the date of the operation on it in my pocket, I felt so strongly repelled by him that I knew that I would never come back and that I would not have an abortion. I no longer wanted to live with the man I was married to, I didn't care for him and he didn't care for the child. The town was strange to me, I knew no one there. My work was strange to me. My mother and sister, whom I loved and was very close to, lived in East Berlin and for a long time I was unable to visit them because after my return to the DDR I was not given the passport necessary for travel to Berlin. Eventually they gave me a provisional document. When I travelled from Neustrelitz to Berlin to see my mother at weekends, all young people were checked in case they might want to disappear to the West. (This was shortly before the Wall was built.) They had to show their identity papers and open up their suitcases. Because I only had a provisional passport I always ended up in a compartment of the train with drawn curtains, where I was questioned. Why did I want to go to Berlin? What was I doing there? They could never believe that I had left the West because I wanted to live in the DDR – it was suffocating. When I read the paper in the mornings I was enraged or ashamed at the lies they told. Nothing was holding me and I left for a second time.

During my first stay in the West I had come to know of a home in Stuttgart, belonging to the church, where single homeless women could have their babies. I travelled to East Berlin, took the train to West Berlin and from there flew to Stuttgart. When I woke up there next morning, the Wall had been built.

Two months later Serjosha was born. We lived in the home, separated except for feeding times. There were about eighty of us women, but over a hundred babies. This was because some of the women had to leave their babies there while they went away to work. Some of us started to look for work in children's homes where we would be able to take our children with us. I ended up in a private children's home in North Germany, by the sea. Serjosha was always parted from me, and while I was dishing out the food for the forty other children, he pulled, clung on to me and screamed. We did not have a room together even though I had made this a condition of accepting the job. I left that place and struggled on with various different jobs. (Bookselling during the day, which meant farming out the child; working in a pub at night, which meant being exhausted the following day; doing paper rounds, and so on.) After a year and a half of that we were both exhausted: exhausted from being parted, exhausted from being together, exhausted from lack of sleep. We were ill, both of us. I thought hard about my situation. There was no chance that things would change – how could they? I went to the Youth Welfare Authority [Jugendamt] and said that I would let my child be adopted by a family. I hoped that this would give him a chance of survival – I didn't think about what would become of me. It all became terrible. I suffered, wanted to cancel the adoption and was told lies. I had no idea what the legal position was at the time. Now I know that it would have been legally possible to retract, but at the time I believed what I was told, that it was impossible.

I lived in Berlin and worked again in a bookshop. In 1968 we formed the first alliance of women, called the Action Group for the Liberation of Women, and because we had realized that women could only work when they knew their children were well looked after we founded children's play groups.

I had only had an elementary school education, so I'd had no chance to go to a polytechnic, and as I wanted nothing more than to learn, to catch up I went back into the tenth grade at school. This would enable me to go on to train as a social worker. I wanted to become a youth worker, but before that I found a job in a remand home for girls. The girls were between fourteen and sixteen years old. During the week they were locked up and not allowed out. They were there because they had too many sisters and brothers and there wasn't enough money or living space at home, so that their parents couldn't manage to hold the whole family together.

I fell in love with a girl, worked there, tried to get the girls out of the home by finding work for them. I didn't know what I ought to do about the love I felt, because above all I felt responsible. By the time I began my social work course I had managed to find jobs for some of the girls in the home.

The teachers on the course used examples of young people in

homes during the post-war years. We never discussed what things were like now – they didn't know and they didn't want to hear about it. They never mentioned, for example, that the girls left the homes with a certificate from a 'Remand Home/ Special School' and that with such a label they would never find a job. They didn't know that the girls, having been locked up for years, were not used to getting by in the outside world. Because of all this I left the college after a year.

I then wrote down everything I had experienced in the home – I had never before written anything longer than a school essay. I wrote fifty pages and gave them to a radio producer who made a sixty-minute programme out of them and put it on the air. As the girls learned nothing in the home and so ended up on the streets, I wrote a programme about prostitution. Then I wrote another about prison, because that was where I found the girls and where I visited them. I wrote down what they said.

In 1969 organizations both big and small were springing up in Berlin. I joined a group of Marxist-Leninists in the Proletarian Women's Centre, and together with eight other women I went to work in a factory. We had sat together on a course and read *Wages, Price and Profit* by Marx, and whenever we asked the lecturers a question about working conditions today they had nothing to say. We wanted to know what conditions were like for women in factories, and what factory work was like. The organization felt that our decision to work in a factory only four weeks after joining was premature and told us to leave it. I stayed put and was consequently expelled from the organization, all the others left the factory. My experience of this organization, with its division into 'activists' and 'subordinates', was terrible. In the mornings when we met in the factory the 'activists' squashed us with the results of the previous night's meeting. They had the knowledge, we didn't. The worst thing was that the 'activists' wanted to work faster on piecework than the women workers they were sitting next to. I was happy when they had all left and I was able to talk to the woman next to me in peace.

I spent five months doing piecework, gave in my notice, and then wrote a description of how we worked and what a day of piecework is like.

I did not know what to do next. I had not joined the organization for fun but because of my experience of the remand home and the women's prison where I had done practical work for my course while I was still at college. I had learned from this that I could not change anything all on my own.

Friends of mine were being searched for, and overnight their faces appeared on posters. The writing underneath said how much the State would pay for their capture. Some of them I had known and loved for many years. When six of the women and men that were sought were betrayed and then arrested in a flat, I took part in finding shelter for the others in order to make life possible for them.

Soon after this they began searching for me. Some of those who were captured later and who couldn't bear the prison tried to save their necks by giving evidence against others. They said that I was with the group, which was true.

In December 1971 I was arrested in a street in Cologne. I was alone and unarmed. Four plain-clothes policemen pointed their guns at me – you are lucky not to get shot dead during the arrest. They kept me in prison for two years. I spent fifteen months of that time in solitary confinement in prisons in Mainz and Anrath. After a trial lasting three months I was released in December 1973.

After I got out I worked in factories in the metal industry. Factories were rationalizing and cutting their workforces furiously during 1974 and 1975, and in that time I was sacked three times. As I was unwilling to let them turn me into a casual labourer, I didn't look for any more work in factories.

Rotbuch Verlag, the Berlin publishing house, were willing to give me enough money to live on for four months, so I sat down to write about my experiences in the factory – tried to find words to describe factory work. *From Hand to Mouth* is the result.

Two years later I worked with a Yugoslavian woman on her autobiography. Her name is Vera Kamenko and she is one of the recruited women, a worker bought for the Federal Republic, on piecework and without her child. While she is imprisoned here in the Federal Republic, she writes her life story. Her German is poor, so we worked together. Her book is called *Unter uns war Krieg* [*Amongst Us – War*].

At the moment I am writing about my experiences in prison, describing what prison is, how you live there. I am doing this because you live in prison with all the same feelings that you have outside, all the feelings of which you are capable.

Marianne Herzog
May 1979

More About Penguins
and Pelicans

For further information about books available from Penguins
please write to Dept EP, Penguin Books Ltd,
Harmondsworth, Middlesex UB7 0DA.

In the U.S.A.: For a complete list of books available from
Penguins in the United States write to Dept CS, Penguin
Books, 625 Madison Avenue, New York, New York 10022.

In Canada: For a complete list of books available from
Penguins in Canada write to Penguin Books Canada Ltd,
2801 John Street, Markham, Ontario L3R 1B4.

In Australia: For a complete list of books available from
Penguins in Australia write to the Marketing Department,
Penguin Books Australia Ltd, P.O. Box 257, Ringwood,
Victoria 3134.

Against Our Will: Men, Women and Rape
Susan Brownmiller

'Rape is nothing more or less than a conscious process of intimidation by which *all men* keep *all women* in a state of fear'. And with this explosive statement, Susan Brownmiller commences her study on rape.

The Feminine Mystique
Betty Friedan

A family and home may constitute the twin heights of female ambition. But how then do you cope with the ever present question of 'Who am I?'.

Housewife
Ann Oakley

A challenge to the conventional set of values which label work a masculine activity and assign woman to unpaid labour in the home.

'Just Like A Girl': How Girls are Taught to be Women
Sue Sharpe

Even in the 1970s, the traditional lot of the working-class girl has changed very 'ittle. Sue Sharpe here shows how society still manages to put bars round girls and women, in upbringing, education and beliefs, both at home and at school.

The Rights and Wrongs of Women
Edited by Juliet Mitchell and Ann Oakley

A serious look at the situation of women and a careful examination of the grounds of female protest, this book covers work, childbirth, political and union activity, education, the home, the concept of equality and the female literary images projected in novels.

Scream Quietly or the Neighbours Will Hear
Erin Pizzey

Assesses the plight of battered wives and the difficulties in setting up houses of refuge to help them.

Woman's Estate
Juliet Mitchell

An examination of the Women's Liberation Movement – the reasons for its growth, its links with other radical protest groups and its aims for the future.

A Vindication of the Rights of Women
Mary Wollstonecraft
Edited by Miriam Kramnick

The first manifesto of the British woman's movement, written in 1792.

Woman's Consciousness, Man's World
Sheila Rowbotham

One of the few studies on the development of the feminine consciousness and the social changes – including the growth of the Woman's Liberation Movement – behind it.

Psychoanalysis and Feminism
Juliet Mitchell

An analysis of sexuality, feminity and the family, as treated in the works of Freud, Reich and Laing.

Women's Rights: A Practical Guide
Anna Coote and Tessa Gill

The definitive guide to what every woman should know about her rights – or lack of them.

Women, Resistance and Revolution
Sheila Rowbotham

A well-documented and wide-ranging survey which charts the roots of sexual inequality and the long sporadic struggle to overcome it.